WAR

The Enemy in the East

ISSUED FORTNIGHTLY BY THE
ARMY BUREAU OF
CURRENT AFFAIRS

No. 14. March 21st, 1942. Not to be Published

Front cover of ABCA 'War' pamphlet No.14

JAPS

British Views on Japan during the Second World War

ARMY BUREAU OF CURRENT AFFAIRS

BooksUlster

First published by the Army Bureau of Current Affairs 1942-45.
This compilation published by Books Ulster in 2016.

Typographical arrangement © Books Ulster

ISBN: 978-1-910375-44-0

Foreword

This publication is a compilation of articles originally published by the (British) Army Bureau of Current Affairs between 1942 and 1945. ABCA was 'created by the Army Council to "brief" officers for talks to their men on war topics and to provide them with informative "background" on varied aspects of the war.' Its *Current Affairs* and *War* series provided the basis for debate within groups of service personnel and each pamphlet contained guidance notes on how the discussion might best be developed. For the most part, except where they prove to be of particular interest, the latter have been excluded from this edition.

The articles have been reproduced in chronological order of publication, but do not necessarily need to be read in that order. 'The Japanese Way' and 'How About Japan?', although they come chronologically later, provide an excellent overview of the history, religion, industry and society of Japan, how it came to be at war with China and the West, and its ultimate objectives.

Other articles focus specifically on the Burma campaign, the Philippines, and Guadalcanal, in the latter of which ('Be mean, and kill' em') there is a series of contributions from US servicemen on their experiences in fighting the Japanese. These were designed primarily as tips to British soldiers yet to face the Imperial Army.

Despite the constant references to 'Japs' and the caricature illustrations of them in a couple of the pamphlets, the overall tone of the material conveys a grudging respect for the Japanese soldier and sympathy with the Japanese people generally. The blame for Japan's aggression is laid firmly at the door of the military who effectively had control of the government and Emperor, although, interestingly, there is acknowledgement of the point that the Western powers may have contributed to the situation by forcing Japan out of its isolation in the 19th Century and consequently from an essentially feudal society into an industrialised one. There is an appreciation too that Japan has to be worked with as a partner in the post-war world, but that the country must necessarily be entirely crushed first.

Many Allied veterans of the Second World War found it understandably impossible to forgive the deprivations and cruelties they suffered at the hands of the Japanese—General Homma himself, who led the Japanese attack on the Philippines, referred to his soldiers not as human beings, but as 'wild beasts from the mountains.' However, others, like Laurens van der Post, author of *A Bar of Shadow*, who became a prisoner of the Japanese in West Java in 1942, were able to show remarkable understanding, compassion and forgiveness. The Japanese soldier had been well-trained to show no mercy, not even to himself, if the occasion arose. He rarely had any choice in the matter. That is made entirely apparent in these essays. But it is also demonstrated that he was subject to the same hopes and fears as his Allied counterparts. One Japanese soldier wrote in his diary about his wife, "I wonder if she is ill and if she is missing me … My comrades flatter me by saying that I am the best shot in the unit. I would like to return safely to Shizuko and tell her this story." The diary had been taken from his corpse.

This collection of contemporary WWII writing gives a truly fascinating insight into how the British Army viewed the war in the Far East and provides an informative range of perspectives on the enemy from the Land of the Rising Sun.

Derek Rowlinson

Contents

WAR

The Enemy in the East

ABCA 'War' Pamphlet No. 14, March 21st, 1942

To all Officers

Information given in WAR is not to be communicated either directly or indirectly to the Press, or to any person not holding an official position in His Majesty's Forces.

WAR is one of the two fortnightly bulletins of ABCA—the Army Bureau of Current Affairs, created by the Army Council to "brief" officers for talks to their men on war topics and to provide them with informative "background" on varied aspects of the war. Contributions and correspondence for WAR should be addressed to the Army Bureau of Current Affairs, Curzon Street House, Curzon Street, London, W.C.1.—and envelopes marked WAR. Contributions may be submitted direct on being initialled by the writer's Commanding Officer. Contributions for Quiz are also invited.

Sequence of Attacks and Landings to the fall of Rangoon

A. Hainan (Feb., 1939).

B. Indo-China (Sept., 1940, and July, 1941).

C. Siam (Dec., 1941).

D. Pearl Harbour (Dec., 1941).

1. Kola Bharu (Dec. 8).

2. Philippines (N. Luzon, Dec. 10).

3. Guam (Dec. 11).

4. Victoria Point (Dec. 15).

5. Miri (Sarawak. Dec. 17).

6. Penang (fell Dec. 19).

7. Davao (Dec. 20).

8. Hong Kong (fell Dec. 25).

9. Kuching (Sarawak. Dec. 28).

10. Manila (fell Jan. 2).

11. Sandakan (Brit. N. Borneo, Jan. 3).

12. Tarakan (Dutch N. Borneo, Jan. 11).

13. Menado (Celebes. Jan. 11).

14. Tavoy (fell Jan. 20).

15. Moulnein area (Jan. 21).

16. Rabaul (N. Britain, Jan. 21).

17. Kieta (Solomons, Jan. 22).

18. Kaviang (New Ireland, Jan. 24).

19. Balik Papan (Borneo, Jan. 25).

20. Kendari (Celebes, Jan. 25).

21. Amboina (Moluccas, Jan. 31).

22. Pontianak (Borneo. Jan. 31).

23. Gasmata (N. Britain, Feb. 8).

24. Macassar (Celebes. Feb. 10).

25. Singapore (fell Feb. 15).

26. Palembang (Sumatra, Feb. 15).

27. Banjermasin (Borneo. Feb. 18).

28. Dili (Timor, Feb. 20).

29. Bali (Feb. 20).

30. Kupang (Timor, Feb. 24).

31. Benkulen (Sumatra, Feb. 27).

32. Bantam, Indramaya and Rembang (Java, Feb. 28).

33. Batavia (Mar. 6).

34. Mindoro (Philippines, Mar. 7).

35. Salamaua (N. Guinea. Mar. 8).

36. Bandoeng (fell Mar. 8).

37. Rangoon (fell Mar. 9).

See map ➜

Japanese invasion and occupation

Supply lines & bases

To Pearl Harbour 3550m.

Ship Routes

The Enemy in the East

THIS is a review of Japan's activities since her successful surprise attack on Pearl Harbour on December 7th. The aim is
to present the recent and current history in the Far East theatre of
war as a comprehensive picture, relating widely-scattered events,
sometimes happening simultaneously, to a single strategic plan.

These notes fall into three parts: first, a summary of Japan's
position and intentions when she launched her attack; second, a
digest of the events as they happened; third, some useful information about the enemy which has emerged during the campaign,
additional to the items on these lines which have already been
published in WAR.

A map showing the sequence of events, etc., is opposite.

I. Intentions

Why Did Japan Go to War?

Briefly because (i) she was faced with deadlock in her four-year-
old war with China, and bitterly resentful of the aid being given
to China by Britain, U.S.A., and Russia; (ii) she was alarmed by
the application of freezing orders against her by Britain, U.S.A.
and the Dutch, following her aggression against Indo-China; (iii)
her economic situation was declining. She either had to give up or
go to war. She did not dare "lose face." Her rulers were a military
clique. She went to war.

Her overtures towards a peaceful settlement in Washington
may have started by being genuine. But they ended by being a
pure, calculated move to gain time and achieve surprise by allay-
ing suspicion of warlike action while her envoys were still in the
American capital.

What Did Japan Seek?

In general terms, Japan's intentions were two-fold: to secure access to raw materials which she did not herself possess; to seek a conclusion to the long-drawn-out war with China by cutting the Burma Road, and so drying up the flow of supplies to the Chinese Armies.

Now look at the drive for possession of the Malayan peninsula in the light of those intentions. The objective was Singapore. To take this British base would give Japan four great advantages in the pursuit of her main aims, as well as fulfilling her part in the Axis world strategy by occupying Allied forces, of all three services, in the Far East. These four advantages would be:

(1) To prevent the Allied fleets from operating in the South China Sea.

(2) To endanger the security of communication between Australia, India, and the Middle East.

(3) To make the position of the Dutch East Indies extremely dangerous and attack on them a natural sequel.

(4) To enable her to operate against Allied shipping in the Indian Ocean, and make a new threat to Burma.

II. Action

Pearl Harbour to Singapore

The attack on Pearl Harbour was the shot aimed at the bull's-eye on a target which included the other islands linking America with the Philippines—Guam, Midway, Wake. Interruption of communications was a first essential in Japan's plan.

The point of the Pearl Harbour attack was that Japan had to strike a blow at the U.S. Navy before launching major combined operations at a distance of 3,500 miles by sea against the two big objectives—the Philippines and Singapore. With the island ring secure Japan could go ahead without having to keep an eye all the time on her eastern flank.

As soon as the lightning blow at Pearl Harbour was registered the next part of the plan went into action.

Japanese troops had been in South Indo-China for six months. They were ready to leap at Siam and the Malay Peninsula. Landings were made in South Siam and North-east Malaya. The drive into Malaya over the Siamese border began. Bangkok, capital of Siam, was entered without delay.

Hong Kong was attacked. Japanese control was established over the International Settlement in Shanghai and other British and American interests in Japanese-occupied China. Air attacks were made on the British Islands of the Gilbert group. The attacks on Luzon (Philippines), Guam, Midway and Wake Islands were pressed home.

Scattered Attacks

By the end of the year—or within three weeks of fighting—Hong Kong was occupied, Japanese forces were established in various parts of the Philippines, and the enemy was pushing hard for the capital, Manila. The Imperial forces were withdrawing, fighting, before heavy odds in Malaya. Penang was evacuated.

On January 2nd Manila was entered, and the defending force under General McArthur concentrated in the Bataan peninsula and in the strongly defended island fortress of Corregidor at the entrance to Manila Bay.

Now the Japanese spread their landings still wider. They attacked the islands off the coast of North Borneo. Kuching, in West Sarawak, with its air base, fell into their hands. The Japanese wanted aerodromes for their coming attacks on the Dutch East Indies.

They landed at Tarakan in Dutch Borneo, aiming at the oil wells (which were destroyed) and at Minahassa in North Celebes, near another important airfield. The air attacks on the Gilbert Islands and Bismarck Archipelago continued.

Attack on Burma

Fighting between British troops in Dutch West Borneo and enemy troops from Sarawak indicated that the Japanese were attempting to push towards other air bases in the island. Japan's plan became even clearer when a large number of transports was reported off Indo-China, indicating the readiness of troops for an attack on Sumatra and Java.

In the week before the Malayan Campaign ended a Japanese force advanced from Siam against South Burma. The enemy was obviously ready to follow up success at Singapore with the next stage of their plan—an attack on Rangoon.

Still more Japanese shipping activity was observed in the Marshall Islands and the bombing of Rabaul (New Britain) made a new attack there seem likely. Operations in Burma were developing daily.

The Enemy's Trend

In the period immediately before the fall of Singapore four tendencies in particular were noted in the enemy's activities:—

(1) Gradual extension of enemy bases south and south-west from Borneo and the Celebes, making a definite threat against the fringe of the Dutch Islands from Sumatra toward Timor.

(2) Continued air operations south and south-east from the Bismarck Archipelago, apparently preliminary to further moves in this area.

(3) Definite indications of an enemy plan to occupy the aerodrome in the Palembang area of Sumatra.

(4) Concentrations at Camranh Bay in Indo-China—probably a general reserve for either Burma or the Dutch East Indies.

Meanwhile in Burma (January 31st) our forces withdrew from Moulmein to the west of the Salween River which now formed our front.

In the Philippines there was little change on the Bataan front, although the enemy had landed replacements for their troops who had undoubtedly suffered heavy casualties.

Dutch East Indies Danger

With the fall of Singapore two things became imminent—large-scale attacks on the Dutch East Indies and increased pressure in Burma where routes were being systematically improved and developed. Japanese forces in transports at sea and ready to sail were logically presumed to have as their objectives the Palembang area of Sumatra and the island of Sumba, which would provide good air and sea bases for an attack on Java.

It was now believed that there were 29 Japanese divisions in the general area of the South China Sea and the Pacific Islands. Heavy pressure against our troops on the southern front in Burma coincided with reports of enemy co-operation with Siamese forces against the northern frontier. At the same time Japanese control in the outer fringe of the Dutch East Indies had continued and Palembang had been occupied after 700 parachute troops were landed.

Sufficient forces were at sea in the area to suggest further operations against the islands east of Java preparatory to the attack on Java itself.

The Pressure Grows

The following week saw steadily increasing activity on all three fronts—Burma, the Philippines and the islands around Java. In Burma our forces were withdrawn behind the Sittang River. Fighting was very heavy and there were considerable casualties on both sides.

On February 19th, in spite of Allied successes against enemy convoys in the area, a force was landed on the island of Bali, where an aerodrome fell into enemy hands. The Japanese landed in Dutch and Portuguese Timor and again the occupation of an aerodrome was reported.

The enemy occupation of southern Sumatra was now almost complete and air activity over Java—especially on the aerodromes in the east and west of the island and on the naval base at Sourabaya—was intensified. The enemy was now able to use bomber bases at many advantageous points, including Palembang, Bali and Rabaul. There was a new extension of Japanese air activity to Australia, where heavy raids were made on Port Darwin.

On the night of February 28th March 1st, despite Allied naval and air attack, the Japanese landed at three points on the north coast of Java—Bantam, Rembang and Indramayu. The landings were made in bright moonlight and under covering fire from warships. Strong infiltrations were made by light mobile columns including cyclists and light tanks. The Allied forces were not re-inforced by land or air, so their air strength dwindled and their numerically inferior land forces were exposed to continual bombing. This was a big factor in the breaking of military resistance. On March 8th Bandoeng, G.H.Q. of the Allies, was captured. At the same time enemy operations in Burma forced our withdrawal from Rangoon.

III. Analysis

Their War Background

In trying to make a sensible, realistic assessment of the Japanese as an enemy it is essential to remember that Japan has been campaigning for the past ten years on the Asiatic mainland. Obviously, the Japanese army has learned valuable lessons by experience in such problems as supply, movement, staff control, and knowledge of the country.

The Japanese are quick and eager to learn new methods—for example, there is their industrialisation, which has been carried from zero to a high degree of modern efficiency in about 50 years. The influx in the Western world of Japanese goods, Japan's vigorous drive to capture the textile trade of the East—these are peace-time instances of the Jap's diligence in learning what is going to profit him. In terms of war, they went to great expense and trouble to send and maintain "missions" to foreign countries, especially the big Powers, in order to keep up to date.

The Japanese ability to mobilise quickly, the racial ability to maintain secrecy, their practical knowledge of countries in which they are operating—these are important factors.

Envelopment Tactics

Japanese skill in major tactics is indisputable and in this war bold planning of large-scale operations have brought success in face of natural obstacles, adverse weather, and often determined opposition. Detailed orders for operations are well carried out if everything goes according to plan, but when the plan is upset during operations considerable delay ensues before steps are taken to meet the new situation.

The Japanese theory of attack is based on envelopment. All their major successes in China have been carried through by this method, but they have rarely succeeded in destroying the opposing force, partly because of faulty holding attacks while the envelopment was in progress and partly because of the Chinese ability to slip out of tight corners.

Tactical errors by junior commanders have consistently caused even their successes to be accompanied by far greater loss than the defensive equipment of the Chinese would warrant.

The Japanese have supreme faith in their own offensive capabilities and are at their weakest when defence or withdrawal is forced on them.

Surprise is their Enemy

Nothing that has happened in the last three months tends to disprove the findings of the Chinese campaign—that the Japanese lack initiative when surprised or found at a tactical disadvantage. Apt to panic if unexpectedly taken at a disadvantage, they will nevertheless quickly rally if not kept on the run.

They show a high standard of training and skill in night operations.

In short, the greatest strength of the Japanese army lies in high morale and plentiful man-power, good security, good training, good staff work, accurate gunnery, and thorough understanding of the principle of "maintenance of the objective," which they will carry out even at the risk of outrunning their supplies.

Their weaknesses, as shown especially in China, have been absence of available reserves for emergency, disregard of flanks and rear, poor minor tactics, lack of speed and initiative in counter-attack, and always the danger that the shock of a reverse would burst the bubble of the "ever-advancing, ever-victorious" army on which their morale is based.

But, as well-trained, confident, tough, well-equipped, determined, modern-minded fighting men they must not be under-estimated.

Notes from Hong Kong

After the fall of Hong Kong, reports by British officers included the following notes:—

Special storm troops formed the spearhead of the attack on Hong Kong. Their armament consisted of Tommy-guns, half-inch machine-guns to pierce shutters or pill-boxes, grenades, a high proportion of long-range mortars which were particularly effective. They wore rubber shoes and used cover skilfully.

Every soldier carried a 1/20,000 map with our positions marked in red and with starting line, route and objective in blue. Their map reading was excellent and most of the officers had "walked the course."

Ammunition was plentiful and reserves were carried by coolies. Stalking, sniping, and mountain tactics, e.g., getting above pill-boxes and defended localities, using trees, were skilfully carried out. When resistance hardened, the Japanese put down severe artillery, dive bombing, mortar and machine-gun support, and then advanced by rushes in parties of ten. The final assault was made with Tommy-guns, showers of grenades and the bayonet.

Their artillery material was inferior. One shell in seven was dud.

Propaganda warfare in the field was used. There were frequent pamphlet raids, and loud-speakers gave subversive broadcasts.

Combined Operations

Regarded as a successful combined operation, the Japanese landing in north-east Malaya yielded some points of interest. The landing was made from three transports between one and two o'clock in the morning at high tide. The sea was very rough and there were many drowning casualties.

Before the main operation began, two landing craft were sent ashore with reconnaissance parties of four engineers, whose task was to fix two guiding lights visible only from the sea. The noise of the surf prevented the detection of these craft. The main landings were made up-creek and were supported by fire from the ships, directed against pill-boxes which were about 15 yards from the top of the beach. M.G. fire from the pill-boxes, plus the heavy barbed wire defences, cost the Japanese heavy losses.

Landing craft were large and small motor boats (60 men and 30 men) and "Yamma"—large-decked sampans for artillery and M.T. The crews of the landing craft—four to six engineers, specially trained—were used after landing for bridging and removing mines.

WAR

Guide for Jap Invaders

ABCA 'War' Pamphlet No. 24, August 8th, 1942

How to Go to War

SINCE Japan entered the war Japanese troops going overseas have been issued with a pamphlet entitled "Read this only and the war is won." Its scope is wide and it is a good example of Japanese thoroughness, with many lessons which apply equally to our own troops. As well as a long catalogue of practical advice, there is an admixture of pep talk and philosophy on the following lines:—

"Five years have passed since the beginning of the China Incident. Over 100,000 comrades have exposed their bones on the continent. The arms of Chiang-Kai-Shek, who killed these comrades, were sold mostly by England and America. Our allies, Germany and Italy, are continuing a battle of death in Europe against England, America and Soviet Russia. America is already assisting England and is essentially participating in the war. For the existence of Japan herself and her obligations to the three-country alliance, not a minute longer must be wasted."

The Need for Oil

As "one of the reasons which necessitate the present military operations" this is given: "Without oil, aeroplanes, warships, mo-tor-cars, etc., cannot move. England and America have captured more than half the world's output, and prohibited its export to Japan. Rubber and tin are essential for military purposes ... the malevolence of England and America has prevented Japan's pur-chasing these materials by just means.

"Japan is confronted with a great mission to briefly put the last finishing blows, as representatives of the Asiatic race, to their invasion of several hundred years. Our incomparable Navy is in full readiness and is infallible; 5-5-3 is the ratio in figures, but, if spirit is added, it is 5-5-7. Moreover, half of the British Navy is finished by Germany. For the Navy now is the best tide. The spirits of hundreds of thousands of warriors are guarding us. The mass for the dead comrades is to win this war.

"While showing our heart-felt thanks to the Navy, who conquered thousands of miles of sea and removed enemy interception, and protected us without sleep and rest, we must fully repay them for their trouble with good war results. We are privileged with an important and honourable mission to fight as representatives of the Asiatic race and to reverse the history of the world, succeeding our glorious history of 2,600 years and for the trust and reliance in us of His Majesty the Generalissimo.

> *"Across the sea,*
> *Corpses in the water,*
> *Across the mountain,*
> *Corpses piling up on the field.*
> *I die only for the sake of the Emperor,*
> *Will never look back."*

Advice on Sailing

So much for the pseudo-theory of the thing, now for the practical advice. The pamphlet says that the most important thing in landing operations is the maintenance of secrecy:—

"There are many instances where a word dropped over a glass of wine in a café just before departure has been the cause of secrets coming to the ears of spies. There is a story of a soldier who landed in South China during the present incident, wrote a letter, and dropped it sealed in a bottle. The letter was carried by the tide to the coast of Korea. What would have been the consequence supposing the letter had reached Vladivostock?

"Be prepared to abandon your dead. Before leaving for the fighting line or, at the latest, on board the ship, make the necessary will and have your hair and nails cut and be ready to die at any time and in any place. Attention must be paid to the following points in order to avoid seasickness:—

(a) Use your will-power and bear in mind the importance of your mission.

(b) When pitching, lie on your side—when rolling, lie on your back.

(c) Fix your eyes on distant things, do not heed the ship's movement.

(d) Divert your mind with games, etc.

(e) Those who are bad sailors: tie up your abdomen and breathe deeply. This is quite effective both on the ship and on small boats. By deep breathing is meant, when the ship goes up, breathe in deeply; when the ship goes down, breathe out deeply; when on a ship do this lying down.

(f) Avoid both a full and an empty stomach. Even if seasick, try to eat a little—not to take food will make one more seasick.

(g) Take sufficient sleep.

(h) A little drink is all right for those fond of drink; drink in excess must be avoided.

(i) Constipation is a most prohibited thing.

"Do keep calm, but the conviction 'I am not going to be seasick' is a most important thing. 'I am getting seasick,' or 'I hope I won't get seasick'—the possessor of such a weak mind is bound to get seasick.

Landing Operations

"As soon as the boats are lowered on to the water, troops commence to trans-ship. For this operation line up in single file, lengthwise, sling your rifle and light machine-gun across the shoulder with a leather belt ... if transfer is difficult, due to high waves, rifles and light machine-guns are to be made into one bundle and packed in a ground sheet ... when descending the rope ladder hold firmly the centre rope, keep the upper part of the body near the ladder, support most of your weight with your arms ... sit cross-legged in your appointed place.

"When the waves are high the boats will sway very much, but they are made so that they cannot capsize under any circumstances. However rough the waves it is quite safe, so remain as you are and keep calm. If you are fired at by the enemy as you approach the shore you should continue to advance and fire at the same time, but, since it is difficult to take good aim owing to the movement of the boat, the firers should choose woods, buildings, hill-tops and other auxiliary objectives in the neighbourhood of the main objective, and they must be ready to fire as soon as they catch sight of the objective when the boat rises on the crest of the wave. When firing with the light machine-gun, bend the body with the motion of the boat.

"While you are braving the enemy's fire, you will gradually approach the shore, then the Platoon Commander will order 'Jump in'; it is most important that you should then jump bravely and confidently, even though the waves are high and the water a little deep. If you wear your life-jacket, it is absolutely safe to jump. Even if it is so deep that you cannot touch bottom when you put a leg down to try, the waves will naturally wash you in and carry you towards the shore; so you must jump in without anxiety and quickly lest you be left behind by the others.

"On the side of the enemy—China and the rest, weaklings all— there will be the clatter of tanks and airplanes assembling. But victory is certain; the only question is how efficiently we can win. We must gauge as quickly as possible the enemy's route, then centre our attack for battle and food supplies. Small numbers of brave men will use the night to infiltrate deep into the enemy lines and so on. The feeling that we are beginning to swallow the enemy is most important.

Living in the Tropics

"Every man, when he finds good water, should refill his flask and it is important to be economical in drinking. It is better when we are suffering from thirst not to drink a lot at one time, but to drink a little often. Also sugar cane, pineapple and coconuts (which contain from one-third to two-thirds of a pint of liquid each) will quench thirst, and in the hills you can cut wistaria and suck the cut place. Wistaria vines contain a great deal of water; cut through the vine near the bottom and place a receptacle under the cut, cut the vine two to three feet higher and the water in the cut portion can be collected.

"Lack of sleep and an empty stomach are the first causes of sunstroke; when it is hot we usually have a bad taste in our mouth and lose our appetite. It is therefore as well to divide our food into several meals and to carry as much red pepper or pickled plums as possible. It is vital even to force ourselves to eat rather than let our stomachs become empty.

"As an example of meals on the march:—

(a) Take half of breakfast before starting and the remainder about two hours after.

(b) Divide lunch into two parts, one at 10.00 hours and the other at 13.00 hours.

(c) Supper can be as usual, but if you are doing a night march it is possible to divide it into not more than two parts.

"Under a strong midday sun very thin garments are bad because they let the sunlight through. Clothes should be as loose as they can and should be worn so as to let the air pass through them as much as possible.

"Owing to the heat, tyres are liable to burst; accordingly when one is likely to be making more than half a day's march there should be inspections before starting and the air pressure reduced to about one-tenth below normal.

Camping in the Tropics

"In the tropics the temperature suddenly drops during the second half of the night, and if we sleep in our clothes, damp with sweat or sea water, it will be the beginning of a cold, therefore we should try to arrange to change our clothes then. The standard of living of the natives is extremely low and knowledge of sanitation none at all, so inhabited areas become nests of fleas, lice, bugs and infectious diseases.

"Accordingly, when using inhabited localities, it is best to make use of Government offices and public halls, and to keep away from ordinary people's dwellings. Against wild animals it is best to light a fire whenever fear of enemy observation does not prevent this; if poisonous snakes are found they must be killed; the liver can be taken (as a medicine) and the flesh roasted and eaten. There is no better tonic than this.

"The bush called mangrove burns quite well while it is still green; the outside of coconuts, the peel of sugar cane and chaff can be used as fuel.

Advice for Battle

"Europeans are dandy but delicate and cowards, therefore rain, mist and night attacks are the things they fear most. They consider night suitable only for dancing, but not for fighting—we must take advantage of this.

"Fighting in intense heat, sweat will get in the eyes; wear a hand towel round the head under the steel helmet and wipe off sweat so as to avoid running into the eyes. Keep the sun at your back. Air is thinner in the hot season, in consequence bullets will travel far. The sun's rays are strong and the colours of things become vivid, consequently marks can be mistaken as being near.

"Travel with speed; where men can pass, cars can surely pass. Break through, even if you have to carry the car."

WAR

Little Men, What Now?

ABCA 'War' Pamphlet No. 37, February 6th, 1943

Little Men, What Now?

By Lieut. RICHARD BENNETT, R.A.

WAR Staff Writer

THE average Japanese soldier stands five foot three, weighs between eight and eight and a half stone, and is far from home. How good is he? At various times he has been underestimated and overvalued. We have been fighting him for over a year. He should by now have emerged from the fog of war as a clearly defined figure. An appreciation is timely. "The period of our defensive attrition in the Pacific is drawing to a close," said President Roosevelt in his message to Congress in January. "Last year we stopped them, but this year we intend to advance."

Before December, 1941, the Japanese soldier and army were like an unsolved mystery story. They eluded accurate analysis. How? For many years the Japanese developed a spy mania that seemed funny at the time, but has since proved effective.

They Give Nothing Away

For 15 years public places were placarded with posters saying not that "Careless Talk Costs Lives," or even that "Walls Have Ears," but more directly "All Foreigners Are Spies." Wireless talks and lectures to workers emphasised the same lesson.

The police trailed all foreigners and kept an accurate dossier of their movements. The foreigner, who never looks remotely like a Japanese, was always conspicuous. As so few foreigners have a thorough knowledge of written and spoken Japanese—three was an estimate for the United States a year ago—the language was almost as good as a secret code. Military observation was confined to the specialised experience of the China War and what could be seen with the eye in Japan. This was rarely more than what the Japanese wanted to show.

The Luck of the Draw

Here are some of the facts that were not concealed. The Japanese Army is conscripted. The population of the main islands is 72 million. The Japanese living in the Empire bring the total up to 100 million. Men are liable for military service between the ages of 17 and 40. Normally conscript service was for two years and men were called up at 20. But conscription was selective and the annual intake was not more than 150,000, and up to 1939 names were drawn by lot from those found fittest to serve. Thus in 1936, the last year for which figures are available, 630,800 conscripts were medically examined. Of these 400,000 fell between what seem to be the equivalent of our grades A1 to B2. The intake was drawn from them. The rest were qualified as fit for various reserves. Only 578 were considered unfit for any type of service. Occupations were represented in the intake in the following percentages: farmers and peasants, 31 per cent.; industrial, 30 per cent.; clerical and commercial, 15 per cent.; teachers, journalists, literary, 5 per cent.; transport, 4 per cent.; and miscellaneous, 15 per cent.

The conscripts' life was not casual. They did not have time to stand around and wonder why they were there. The barracks were also a school where they were taught unquestioning devotion to the Emperor, the invincibility of the Japanese Army, and the inferiority of all foreigners. Life was serious. Their service began with a ceremony. The Mayor of their town made a speech to them before they left. Many of them reported for duty accompanied by crowds of relatives. The colonel, too, made a speech: "You will see that these sons of yours will be nurtured by the Army," he told them. "They will be given the courage to leap like lions upon the foe."

A routine like the issue of rifles was dramatised. The major made a speech about it. Each man as he was called out bowed before the rifle in the major's hand, took it, bowed again and returned to the ranks.

"Manœuvres are War"

Pay was about 10s. a month, and of this 8s. was stopped for dependents' allowance and 1s. 9d. for compulsory saving. Conscripts can squander the odd 3d. as they please. To-day, troops in the S.W. Pacific may be paid twice or three times as much. They were not encouraged to be smart, but they were made to be tough. The training was hard. Here are two examples recorded by Lieut.-Colonel Harold Doud, an American officer who was attached for six months to the Japanese 7th Infantry Regiment. A company commander marched his men back 25 miles from a two-day exercise and doubled them three times round the square to show them that "they were not as tired as they thought they were." A whole company was kept on night patrols during manœuvres, and their officer explained, "They already know how to sleep. They need training in how to keep awake." Another American officer reports men being doubled after marching back from manœuvres 122 miles in 72 hours. He suggested that this was extreme for manœuvres. "Manœuvres are war as far as I am concerned," said the Japanese commander.

Now for some questions to which the Japanese do not supply the answers. How many of these peace-time conscripts are in the Pacific battle-fronts? The regular Japanese Army was about 320,000 strong, it was increased by 50,000 in 1931 at the time of the conquest of Manchuria, and at the beginning of the Chinese War in 1937 could call upon two to two and a half million trained reserves. Mobilisation has proceeded steadily since.

There may now be approximately 90 divisions, each on an average 20,000 strong. There are also about 15 tank regiments, of not more than 150 tanks each, and five or six cavalry brigades.

Adding army, corps, and line of communications troops, gives a total of 2,500,000. This is a purely provisional estimate. It is by no means as large an army as Japanese man-power would allow. The indications are that Japan, at the moment, is mobilising the maximum amount of industrial strength. Losses in killed and captured since 1937 have been estimated at about 500,000.

Where are They?

How are these forces disposed? This question, too, must be answered in general terms. Look at the problem through Japanese eyes. First they have the five-year-old China war on their hands. Secondly, they have a scattered front from the Bay of Bengal to the extremes of the South-West Pacific; thirdly, there is the possibility of war with Russia. About this time last year responsible but unofficial British and American estimates gave the Japanese 20 divisions in China, 25 on the Pacific front, and 30 facing the Russians in Manchuria. Assuming these figures to be approximately correct, there would certainly have been some redistribution since then, and calls will now be made on Japanese man-power by the Pacific, Manchurian and Chinese fronts in that order of precedence. But it is not likely that the Manchurian army has been drastically reduced. The well-armed Far Eastern Red Army would be a much more formidable opponent than the brave but inadequately equipped Chinese. The Japanese have already had two unsuccessful trials of strength with the Russians, first in the battle of Changkufeng in the summer of 1938, and again with even less success at Nomonhan in the following year. They learned to respect them. The bulk of Japan's tank force is said to be concentrated in Manchuria.

What Have They Got?

Where did the Japanese learn their military science? Some experts declare that Japan is the Germany of the Far East, and that the Japanese army is modelled on the German. The Japanese

What Japan has gained since December 1941
Per cent of World production

	10	20	30	40	50	60	70	80	90	100

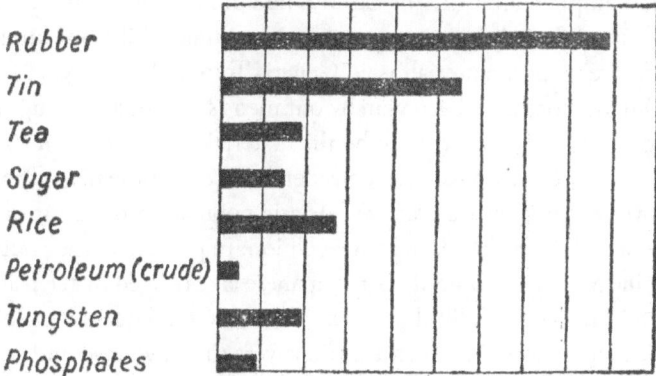

Rubber
Tin
Tea
Sugar
Rice
Petroleum (crude)
Tungsten
Phosphates

This does not take into account the amount destroyed by "Scorched earth policy."
From "An A B C of the Pacific," by Dorothy Woodman, Penguin Books.

have borrowed ideas from the Germans as from everyone else, but there is no other basis for this popular belief, and Japanese armament shows signs of French rather than German influence. Other experts have declared that Japan is so weak industrially that she should be called the Italy of the Far East. This is an exaggeration based on Japan's need to import nearly all industrial raw materials before the war. Conquest has since made good many of these deficiencies. Look at the diagram above.

It is true, however, that Japanese armament is inferior both in quality and quantity to that of its opponents outside China. The divisional establishment of M.T. is low by European or American standards, but legs are more useful than wheels in the country in which they are campaigning. Japanese aircraft are not as good as our best, but are very manœuvrable and have long ranges. It is reported that only enough are being built to replace losses. Thus Japan's industrial capacity is certainly puny compared with our own and the American. It carries with it the seeds of future weakness and defeat.

"A Long-drawn-out Affair"

It is, however, also true that the Japanese seem to have designed and equipped an army for exactly the kind of war she has been fighting. "We rely upon men and their training, while the United States rely upon material," said General Tojo, in February, 1942. "Our victories have been won by our men's superior skill in fighting and courage rather than by the material in our possession."

Their victories have been considerable. Look at the map. Their power extends over a scattered Asiatic population of about one and a half times that of the Soviet Union. In particular, the South China Sea has become almost a Japanese lake fringed by territory rich in resources. Will they have time to consolidate and exploit this empire? Are they as sure as they were that it will expand still further? Listen again to the voice of General Tojo nine months later. "Great East Asia has now emerged from the first stage which was full of surprise attacks and blitzkriegs, and has now become a long-drawn-out affair."

How has the Japanese soldier taken to the change?

Japanese tactics and the fighting qualities of their soldiers in the first three months of lightning success have already been covered in WAR No. 14 (March 21st, 1942). Are they as good on the defensive?

"They Kill or Get Killed"

Here is a recent estimate from an American Marine officer serving in the Solomons:—

"Individually he (the Japanese soldier) is a good soldier; in fact, an excellent one. They very, very seldom give up but will fight until killed, even after being badly wounded. Of a force of well over 700 that we wiped out we were only able to take 34 prisoners, and 33 were so badly wounded that they couldn't do anything. We asked each one if they had been told that they would be killed if captured, and they said 'No.' All insisted that

An Asiatic Empire takes shape: Where they were and where they are they would never be able to return to Japan, so that probably is the answer. ...

"The ones that were wounded would be perfectly still but continued to snipe at us all during the day. We had one captain wounded by one even after we had, we thought, cleaned them out thoroughly. As we closed in through the mass of bodies, one man happened to step on a hand, and he thought he felt it move, so he kicked it. As he did the Jap jumped up and tried to throw a grenade at a group near, but the pin never came out. I actually saw dead Japs with grenades in their hands with the pins pulled. Others I saw had two or three wounds that had been bound up, but they stayed there right until the end. After it was all over we saw one swimming well out to sea, so we sent a boat out to get him. As the boat came alongside he made a dive and never came up. In other words, they kill or get killed, you must give them that credit."

The Next-of-kin are Not Told

Nor was this exceptional. Reports from Tulagi, Gona and other battlefields tell the same story. The Japanese soldier is trained to fight to the last man and the last round. "From now on, the occupying operation of Guadalcanal is under the observation of the whole world," reads a Japanese order of the day. "Do not expect to return, not even one man, if the operation is unsuccessful." The Japanese Government is not interested in receiving the names of prisoners of war, nor does it communicate them to the next of kin. The official attitude is that so far as the Government or the families are concerned prisoners are dead.

The job of clearing the Japanese from every island on which they have a foothold will not be quick or easy.

But, despite his high morale, the Japanese has not recently been attacking with the frenzied neglect of life that some earlier reports have suggested. Here is an Australian appraisal: "When attacking an objective, the Japanese was bold and persistent. He attacked again and again, plunging more men into successive attacks. He was not ordered to do unreasonable feats, as is often suggested by accounts of the fanatical spirit of self-sacrifice accredited to him. On the contrary, he generally hammered at the weak spot. His forward troops in approach appeared more skilled than his average soldiers. Generally, however, bunched formations were not uncommon during the attack proper."

Report of suicidal exploits by Japanese airmen can also be discounted. They show skill and courage, but do not throw their lives away except to avoid surrender. Thus it is considered bad form for an airman to be strapped to his parachute when flying over enemy territory. There is no separate Japanese air force, but an Army Air Force and a Naval Air Force. Both have been used in close co-operation with the army.

Organisation and planning have worked well. Japanese administration has been simple and effective, and relies almost entirely on verbal orders. Supply has been generally good in spite of the great difficulties. The ration, the basis of which is rice, on analysis has a low total energy value by European standards. It is rich in vitamins A, B and D, and deficient in C. The sappers are first class and have cleared bombed aerodromes and repaired demolished bridges in a shorter time than was thought possible. Concealment and camouflage are excellent. In the Solomons snipers have been issued with a net which makes them invisible at 50 yards.

They Have Their Weak Points, Too

The Japanese soldier has been good, but he has not been perfect. His tendency to panic when things go wrong has already been noted in WAR. He has not been psychologically or militarily prepared for defence or retreat, and quickly becomes browned off and despondent, even after quite small reverses. The airmen are reported to be a little wooden in their lack of initiative. On bombing sorties not all pilots are briefed. They follow their leaders. If the leaders are shot down the raid is liable to become a scattered failure. The performance of single aircraft over enemy territory where there are no Japanese spectators is less dashing than where there are.

Here is a picture of Marines under fire. After a small air-raid on Guadalcanal, a Japanese Marine wrote in his diary: "Several bombs were dropped; however, there was no damage. Even though there is no damage, the bombing is very dreadful. The workers seem to scatter like small spiders directly the alarm goes. Even the soldiers have it in mind to flee as they watch the enemy planes. The higher officers would flee before anybody else."

"It is Not Fun Any More"

The Americans landed and the bombing grew worse. The nerves of those in command began to get jagged. "To-night the platoon leader is in a bad mood," wrote another Marine, "and is criticising everything. During supper 1st Class man Matshi received a stern glance five times and uncomplimentary remarks as if he would strike him."

They were waiting for reinforcements. "It is not fun any more," is the comment. "I believe the Navy doesn't care about us here." And later, "Do they know we are left on this island or don't they? The lack of sympathy by the headquarters is too extreme. The reinforcements are completely annihilated. Where is the mighty power of the Imperial Navy? It is too regretful." Two days later. "The morale of our forces is going down. It seems as if we have lost our hostile intention." They meditated on death. One wanted to go out and die gloriously for his country after "overpowering 3 to 5 enemy soldiers"; another "To go back to Japan to set out again as a soldier and die for my country." To die on the defensive and in defeat was not what he had been led to expect. One at least wanted simply to go back and not set out again. He was worried about his wife Shizuko. "I wonder if she is ill and if she is missing me," he wrote. "My comrades flatter me by saying that I am the best shot in the unit. I would like to return safely to Shizuko and tell her this story." He did not. They were demoralised but the possibility of surrender did not occur to them.

They would probably have retreated if it had been possible, as other Japanese troops have retreated, and the retreat might have become a rout as may happen when the Japanese start a backward movement contrary to all their military belief and training. But they did not live to spread their demoralisation. They were cornered and they died.

Trouble About Initiative

Regimental officers, too, have shown serious weaknesses. Foreign observers consider that they show a lack of initiative when faced with an unexpected situation. This seems to have been true. Senior Japanese officers, however, consider that they show too much initiative in disobeying superior orders. This also seems to have been true. This disobedience became so widespread in the Burma campaign that one divisional commander had to issue a warning to his officers not to depart without reason from his orders. Nor does the position seem to have improved since. A second lieutenant who had been ordered to carry out a night attack on Guadalcanal, notes with satisfaction, "As contradiction occurred successively in the divisional order, the detachment order and the regimental order, we suspended the night attack on the agreement of Unit Commander Tamura and Unit Commander Usui." Three days later they disobeyed another order for a night attack. "I thanked Major Tamura," he wrote, "for his proposal to cancel the night attack, which was contrary to the fundamental rule of combat, to avoid the useless loss of troops. To be killed by enemy gunfire and bombing without inflicting losses on them is not the intention of military men."

£7 a Week for a General

Refusal to carry out counter-attacks to retrieve a difficult situation does not argue a high morale among military men. Its implications are serious. Does experience in Guadalcanal show that Japanese morale is linked to the belief in Japanese invincibility? It may be. But it is too early to say that one automatically collapses with the other.

Apart from alternating between too much or too little initiative, the officers are otherwise conscientious and efficient. They are mostly, but not all, from the middle classes, and have served in the army since the age of 17. There is no longer a rigid military caste in Japan. The army is a people's army. Officers are poorly paid by Western standards. A general draws about £7 a week. Discipline in units is good. There is hardly any military crime on duty. Off duty the Japanese soldier qualifies for the two conventional soldierly epithets. Rape, looting, and atrocious violence, if not encouraged by officers, is certainly not prohibited or punished. Nor are the officers models themselves. Incidence of venereal disease is high among all ranks.

A Long Journey Either Way

What are the conclusions? In defence or retreat the Japanese is not so skilful or formidable as in victorious advance. When his faith has been sapped, his morale may crack. In a long war the superior mass of our equipment will eventually be felt. These are possible factors that may affect the fighting on the Asiatic mainland. On the islands, when the Japanese soldier is cornered and must surrender or die he is not likely to surrender. Winkling them out of the South seas will be a hard and bloody business.

How wholeheartedly are the Japanese in the war? There may be Japanese who oppose their country's imperial ambitions. There were once, but mass arrests and repression have reduced their numbers, and enforced secrecy and silence on the survivors. The services do not tolerate internal opposition. The War Minister is always a general on the active list. The Government does not intervene in military affairs, but the army plunges into politics, and as often as not with the assassin's knife. The men directing the

Japanese war effort have a plan. It is briefly to conquer the world.

They have a long way to go if they are to get there. They have a long way to get back if they don't.

WAR

"Be mean and kill 'em"

ABCA 'War' Pamphlet No. 41, April 3rd, 1943

Guadalcanal

How it happened

The background of the operations covered in this bulletin is that about the beginning of last July a Japanese force was landed on Guadalcanal. They were to build an airfield which could provide fighter cover for their own shipping, and act as a base for air attacks on United Nations' shipping.

American forces landed on August 7th, 1942, and against stubborn Japanese resistance, captured the airfield, which they named Henderson Airfield. They then drove a wedge between the Japanese forces, the greater part of which were driven westward. Smaller parties withdrew eastward and were later mopped up. The larger part were hemmed into the north-west part of the island (see map), where most of them were killed or taken prisoner, and the rest evacuated. By mid-February, 1943, the American forces were in possession of Guadalcanal.

To secure the point of view of the fighting men in this theatre, Lt.-Col. Russel P. Reeder, Jr., of the Operations Division of the United States War Department General Staff, was sent to Guadalcanal by General Marshall, United States Chief of Staff, who writes in a foreword:—

"The stories of these men as told to Colonel Reeder have been printed for your information. The American marines and doughboys show us that the Jap is no superman. He is a tricky, vicious, and fanatical fighter. But they are beating him day after day. Theirs is a priceless record of the gallantry and resourcefulness of the American fighting man at his best.

"Soldiers and officers alike should read these notes and seek to apply their lessons. We must cash in on the experience which these and other brave men have paid for in blood."

"Be mean, and kill'em"

" I BEEN in the Marines 16 years, and I been in three expeditions to China and five engagements since I have been in the Solomons. I will say that this new model recruit we are getting can drink more water than six old-timers. We have to stress water discipline all the time. They don't seem to realise what real water discipline is. We have too many N.C.O.s in the Marines who are 'namby-pamby' and beat around the bush. Our N.C.O.s are gradually toughening up and are seeing reasons why they must meet their responsibilities. Respectfully speaking, sir, I think that when officers make a N.C.O. they should go over in their minds 'what kind of N.C.O. will he make in the field.'"

Gunnery-Sergeant H. L. Beardsley.

Later They were Sorry

"Some of my men thought their hand grenades were too heavy. They tossed them aside when no one was looking. Later they would have given six months' pay for one hand grenade.

"I hear that in the new jungle kits the men will get water steril-ising tablets. These will help, as my men dip water out of streams."

Pln.-Sgt. H. R. Strong.

By Moving in Fast

"After the Japs had been located, my platoon has gained the element of surprise by moving in fast with bayonets and hand grenades.

"In turn, they have surprised us by being in a defensive posi-tion on the reverse slope of a ridge. I think the snipers look for automatic rifle men." (Note by Col. Edson: "No doubt about this. In one engagement, in one platoon, every automatic rifle man was hit.")

Pln.-Sgt. F. T. O'Fara.

I Got Within Four Feet

Sir, I would like to tell you that a man's keenness or dullness of eye may determine whether or not he will live. Ten men in my platoon were killed because they walked up on a Jap 37mm. gun. I went up later, after the gun had been put out by our mortars, to help bring back the dead. The Japanese gun was so well camouflaged that I got within four feet of the gun before I saw it."

Pln.-Sgt. R. A. Zullo.

Confused at Night

"I hate to admit it, but it's the truth; when we got here a lot of our young men were confused at night. They were not used to jungle at night. They could not use their compasses at night, and we did not have enough compasses.

"We have learned that when we get off the beaten trails it seems to confuse the Japs, and we have better success."

Marine Gunner E. S. Rust.

Help Overcome Ambush Fire

"When we move around on these jungle trails we have learned to have men at the rear of each platoon who carry light loads so they can get their weapon into action quickly to help overcome ambush fire from the rear.

"Some of our new men were so scared of our hand grenades when they were first issued that they jammed down the cotter pin. Then, later in action, they could not pull the pin.

Pln.-Sgt. J. C. L. Hollingsworth.

Too Much High Firing

"Unnecessary firing gives your position away, and when you give your position away here, you pay for it.

"It's helpful in using the field glass in this tropical sun to cup your hand over the front end in order to keep out the glare.

"The men in my squad fire low at the base of the trees. There is too much high firing going on. I have observed the Japs often get short of ammunition. They cut bamboo and crack it together to simulate rifle fire to draw our fire. They ain't supermen; they're just tricky bastards.

"A palmetto log looks sturdy for use in machine gun emplacements and dugouts, but it is spongy and rots. I have seen it collapse and pin the gun. It is better to use the hard wood."

Cpl. J. S. Stankus.

A Good Jungle Knife

"We are learning the hard way to move quietly in this jungle.

"I have been fired at many times by snipers and haven't seen one yet.

"The sabres which the Japanese officers carry have proved to be worthless. I killed two Japs who came at me with sabres and I got them first by shooting them. But, I wished I had 'in reserve' a good jungle knife. I don't mean a bolo, which we should have for cutting trails, but a knife with a 12-inch blade of good steel. We could use this against these Japs as well as cutting vines that catch on us at night." (Note: Many men expressed their wish for a jungle knife such as described here. This desire is being omitted in further remarks to avoid repetition.)

Pln.-Sgt. C. M. Feagin.

We are Curing Ourselves

"On the Matanikau River we got to firing at each other because of careless leadership by the junior leaders. We are curing ourselves of promiscuous firing, but I should think new units would get training to make the men careful.

"*We learned not to fire unless we had something to shoot at. Doing otherwise discloses your position and wastes ammunition.*

"Sergeant Dietrich of Company I, of our Regiment, recently used his head. One night when the Japs advanced, a Jap jumped into Sergeant Dietrich's fox hole. Sergeant Dietrich pulled the pin of a hand grenade and jumped out. There was a hell of an explosion and one less Nip.

"I have been charged twice by the Japs in bayonet charge. *Our Marines can out-bayonet fight them and I know our Army men will do the same.* (Note by Col. Edson: 'Incidentally, in the last push we executed three bayonet charges.')

"A Japanese trick to draw our fire was for the hidden Jap to work his bolt back and forth. Men who got sucked in on this and fired without seeing what they were firing at, generally drew automatic fire from another direction.

"Every scout should be taught to look in the trees. I was a scout and got shot in the shoulder by a Jap in a tree. I look in the trees now.

"We take turns being scouts; so, all should be trained as scouts."

Cpl. Fred Carter.

Help Him by Pushing Ahead

"You crawl in the advance—unless you are to charge and make it. The reason for this is that all men hit are hit from the knees up, except for ricochets. We have crawled up to within 25 yards of a machine gun firing over our backs. The Japs don't depress their machine guns. (Note by Col. Edson: 'I saw men of Company L doing this.')

"Men get killed rushing to help a wounded man. If the wounded man would crawl about ten yards to his flank, he can generally be aided to safety, as the Japs seem to fire down lanes in the jungle. (Remark by Col. Edson: 'We have taught our men that the best way to aid a wounded man is to push ahead so that the wounded man can be cared for by the Corps Men.')

"The men have to be trained individually, for when the fight starts, the Corporal can't see all of his men and further, when the order for attack is given, any number of men are unable to see the man on his right or left. So you see, Sir, it takes guts for men to get up and move forward when the signal is given. The men have to depend on one another and have confidence in each other.

"I was in one advance when the Japs let us come through and then rose up out of covered fox holes and shot us in the back. The best cure for that is a rear guard looking towards the rear."

Sgt. O. J. Marion.

Weird Noises at Night

"Get used to weird noises at night. This jungle is not still at night. The land crabs and lizards make a hell of a noise rustling on leaves. And there is a bird here that sounds like a man banging two blocks of wood together. There is another bird that makes a noise like a dog barking. I thought, Sir, this might give you an idea for your training."

Cpl. E. J. Byrne.

A Commanding Officer's Report

"If I had to train my regiment over again, I would stress small group training and the training of the individual even more than we did when we were in training.

"There must be training in difficult observation, which is needed for the offence. It is my observation that only 5 per cent. of the men can really see while observing.

"The offensive is the most difficult to support, as you cannot tell exactly where your troops are.

"Whether the Japs will continue to fight as they do now, I don't know. They defend on the low ground in the jungle. They dig standing trenches, extremely well camouflaged.

"We need the rifle grenade, or a weapon to fill the gap between hand grenade and the mortar. We need to dig the Nip out of his hole under banyan trees, etc.

"The tendency is to overload the infantrymen with ammunition. It seems to be the standard practice to start out with a belt full plus two bandoliers. We soon found out that 25 rounds was enough for two or three days if you do not have targets to shoot at. (Note.—Our infantrymen approaching Buna in the jungles of New Guinea were carrying 40 rounds.)

"Two ammunition pockets in the belt should be converted to grenade pockets. Each man should have two hand grenades. If you don't do that, develop slip-open pockets, which can be quickly opened and which will carry two hand grenades.

Snipers are Annoying

"In your scouting and patrolling, and your 'training in patience' (which you should have) have the men work against each other. Same thing for squads and platoons in their problems.

"We should develop better snipers. The Japanese snipers are really annoying. All commanders must realise you cannot clear out all the snipers before you advance. Some will be left, but they won't be particularly effective. Annoying, yes. You can get these snipers by small groups from the reserves. Some Japanese snipers, which were by-passed in the attack, hid for two or three days and then quit. Some will hang around inside your lines for a month.

"The Japanese night attacks, of course, have limited objectives; and sometimes withdrawing after dark as much as 50 yards will fool them and they won't know where you are.

"In the Raiders we adopted the custom of dropping all ranks and titles. We used nicknames for the officers. All ranks use these nicknames for us. We did this because the Nips caught on to the names of the officers and would yell or speak in the night, 'This is Captain Joe Smith talking. 'A' Company withdraw to the next hill.' So we adopted nicknames as code words. Captain Walt became 'Silent Lou.' My nickname was 'Red Mike.' An example of the use of these nicknames as code words is: One night the Japs put down smoke and they yelled 'gas.' We were green at that time and two of our companies withdrew leaving A Company exposed on its two flanks. In this instance I was a battalion commander. Captain Walt called me on the voice radio to inform me of the situation. He was cautious and used the nickname as follows: He said, 'Who is speaking?' and I said, 'Red.' He said, 'What name do you identify with "Silent"?' I said, 'Lou.' He said, 'That is correct.' So, we both knew that we were talking to each other and were not talking to the enemy. He explained the situation to me. At the end of his conversation, a voice broke in and said in perfect English, 'Our situation here, Colonel Edson, is excellent. Thank you, sir.' This was the enemy speaking.

Learn the Normal Noises

A value of night training is that it lets men learn the normal noises of the woods at night. Woods are not silent at night.

"The Japanese is no superman. He has the same limitations that we have. They have the advantage of experience. With proper training, our Americans are better, as our people can think better as individuals. Encourage your individuals and bring them out.

"Both our riflemen and machine-gunners must be taught to shoot low.

"This leadership business resolves itself down to being hard-boiled. By that I mean getting rid of the poor leader, even if you like him personally, because this is a life and death affair. This goes right on down to the non-coms.

"At Tulagi the Japanese used wooden bullets. I saw some of these wooden bullets. My theory for their use is that they were developed for troops which were to infiltrate behind our lines and shoot us in the back. These wooden bullets could not carry far enough to injure attacking troops."

Col. Merritt A. Edson.

How They Broke Out

"We had nine men killed in one company in the last assault. Four of these men were killed by a wounded sniper who had three holes in him. He was laying in thick brush 15 yards from my CP. He was camouflaged and had been passed over for dead. You have to *kill* to put them out. They attack in bunches, shoulder to shoulder. An example: We were on the Matanikau River (see Fig. 1). Our companies were at half strength. This was a Raider Battalion plus two companies of the 3rd Battalion, Fifth Marines. The Japanese beach head was a thick jungle with camouflaged standing-type fox holes. They had with them in their beach head six heavy machine-guns and eight light machine-guns which we captured in this action.

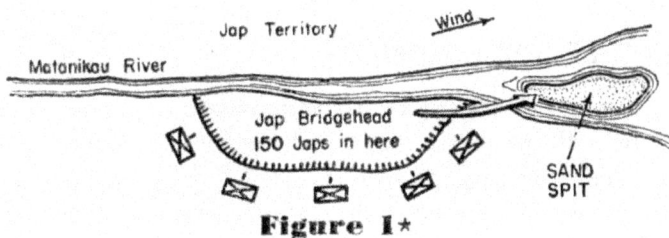

Figure I ★

★ American conventional signs.

"At 6.30 p.m. they smoked our two right companies, and when the smoke had enveloped these two companies, they broke out. They came out in a mass formation, 20 abreast, yelling, bayonets fixed, automatic weapons working, rear ranks throwing hand grenades (heavy arrow in the sketch shows the Japanese route). They were trying to escape to the sand spit at the mouth of the river in order to cross the river to get back. Our right front company had just completed a double-apron barbed-wire fence. When the Japanese hit the left flank of the right company, they killed nine out of the first 11 men they met. Then they hit the barbed wire. Two of our heavy machine-guns opened up, shooting down along this barbed-wire fence and dispersed their attack. It got dark—quickly, like it does here. There was smoke, Japs and Marines all mixed up. Three Jap officers were swinging their two-hand swords. There was hand-to-hand fighting all night long. We mopped them up at daybreak. We killed 78 Japs. They killed 12 Marines and wounded 26 of us.

"The Jap has a great deal of respect for our hand grenade, and it is a valuable weapon to us. *Do you ever practise throwing it in wooded country?*

Major Lou Walt.

They Laughed, but Look Now

"I practise walking quietly over rocks, twigs, grass, leaves, through vines, etc. I practise this around this bivouac area. I received instructions in scouting and patrolling at Quantico, but I still practise this around here in the bivouac area. I believe because I practise this is the reason I am still alive. Some of the other N.C.O.s laughed at me because I am always seeing how quietly I can walk around and because I go out and practise on my own. But they have stopped laughing, because I have been on more patrols than any man in the regiment, and I am still alive.

"When I am scouting and come to an opening in the jungle, and have to cross it, I generally run across quickly and quietly. Going slow here may cost a scout his life. Different types of terrain call for different methods.

"Here is the way Japs patrol. I was out on the bank of the river with another man. We were observing, and were carefully camouflaged. We heard a little sound, and then saw two Japs crawl by about seven feet away from us. These Japs were unarmed. We started to shoot them, but did not do so as we remembered our mission. Then, 15 yards later came eight armed Japs. They were walking slowly and carefully. We did not shoot, as our mission was to gain information. When I got back we had a lot of discussion as to why the two Japs in front were not armed. Some of the fellows said maybe it was a form of Japanese company punishment. I believe they were the point of the patrol, and were unarmed so they could crawl better.

"You can tell Jap troops in the distance by their short, choppy step." (Remark by Col. Edson: "This is true, and we think the reason for their short, choppy stride is because they wear wooden shoes in Japan.")

Pln.-Sgt. C. C. Arndt.

Here is an Example

"Is the Army stripping down to essentials in equipment?

"Teach not to waste ammunition. Learn to make every shot count.

"Don't spare your artillery. Make the most of it. Every time you get enough information, even if the target is not profitable, get artillery fire on it. They hate it.

"Try to get the Japs on the move; keep bouncing them around; don't let them get set. When you let them get set they are hard to get out. We have had a great deal of success with the 81 mm. mortar and with artillery fire. Here is an example (see Fig. 2).

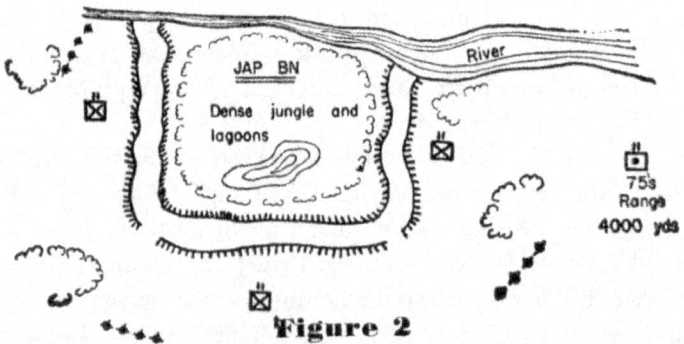

Figure 2

"We have the Japs surrounded with their backs to the river. The three battalions were in close contact with the enemy. It was obvious that we had a large number of Japs surrounded, and that the best way to get them out was to place field artillery and 81 mm. fire on them. However, the problem was to put this fire on the enemy, and not on our own troops. The movement which we executed was carefully co-ordinated with the artillery and with the mortars. Each battalion, at a certain time, was to withdraw just before the firing was due to start. *We were very careful to explain to the men what we were doing so that they would not get a mistaken idea of the order for withdrawing.* The manœuvre was successful. Over 500 Japs were killed in this action. We had 44 Marines killed and 63 wounded. Our men were not hurt by the artillery and mortar fire, of course, but were killed and wounded in the fighting which took place before the withdrawal. After the firing ceased we went in and mopped up in hand-to-hand fighting.

"Our orders to our Marines on the perimeter defence are: 'You stay on your position and do not pull back. If they bust through you we'll plug up the hole, but you stay there.'

"This regiment can out-yell the Japs, out-fight them, out-bay-onet them, and out-shoot them. This yelling, as in hand-to-hand action, is important. It is like a football team.

"The Japs yell at us: 'Marines, we're gonna keel you! More blood for the Emperor!' The Marines yell back: 'You — — — —. We'll kill you Japs. More blood for Franklin!'

"The regimental commander must make it his personal duty to watch and be greatly interested in sanitation; our sick list is lower than normal. Our sick list runs lower than 40 men per battalion."

Colonel Amor Le R. Sims.

Thought They Were Safe

The following is the result of a conference with five N.C.O.s selected by Lt.-Col. Puller:

"The Japanese fire is not always aimed. It is harassing fire and scares recruits. Get the recruits so they are used to overhead fire. Japs who have infiltrated signal to each other with their rifles by the number of shots. We get these birds by constant patrolling.

"The snipers tie their guns in the trees so they can't drop it carelessly or if wounded. In putting their light machine-guns in the trees, they lash them in and have relief men ready to go up the tree.

"Their machine-guns don't traverse and search."

A Jap trick:

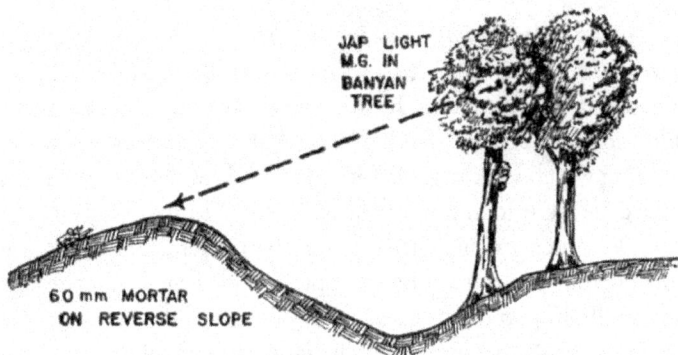

JAP LIGHT
M.G. IN
BANYAN
TREE

60 mm MORTAR
ON REVERSE SLOPE

Figure 3

The mortar men thought they were safe. The Japanese let them fire two or three rounds. They cracked down, killed three and wounded two.

"The rifle grenade demoralises the Jap. A Japanese prisoner told me in English, 'That 30 calibre cannon is terrible, Sir.' The Japanese sew grass and leaves to their shirts and hats.

"They hit hell out of our points. They don't wait until they could get more men. They seek to delay us. When the point goes down, teach men to get behind big trees, if close, but not behind saplings.

"If you shoot their officers, they mill around. Their N.C.O.s are poor. You can tell they are officers by their sabres and leather puttees.

"A lot of these Japs who infiltrate have radios. Think of this advantage in respect to artillery, mortar fire, location of troops, etc.

"My platoon found nine Japs slipping behind our lines. (Note by Lt.-Col. Frisbee, Regimental Executive officer: 'We have killed 38 Japs behind our lines during the period of August 7th, 1942, to November 28th, 1942.')

"Their outpost at times is in trees. I saw one tree which was rotten inside. The Japanese had a light machine-gun and gunner down inside, and they had built a trap door on our side. Every once in a while the door would open, and they would poke the machine-gun out and fire. We took care of this.

"When we cease firing, they cease firing. When we fire, they open up. They do this to conceal their positions."

Are Snipers Over-emphasised?

"Sir, the first thing I would like to say is that this Japanese sniper business has been over-emphasised. They talked and talked to us about the Japanese snipers and made these young men of mine jittery. You can't see the sniper anyhow until you start to attack, and as his fire, until the attack starts, is very inaccurate, there is no use to worry. I think this sniper business should be debunked. They hide under banyan trees and just poke their muzzle through a hole and fire, indiscriminately. When the attack starts, they will come out. Those you by-pass in the attack must be mopped up later.

"We learned not to get excited or go off half-cocked where there is noise. The Japanese make noise to mislead us. They shot off some fire crackers at the start, but we have learned that where the noise is, he ain't. You never hear him move. He sleeps in the daytime and does his work at night.

"We learned to dig *small* covered fox holes. Slit trenches are best. We had men smothered to death in too large holes. Don't put more than three men in any hole unless the hole has a support on top big enough to stop a 500lb. bomb.

"Teach the young fellows to look over the ground and look in the trees and to learn where the enemy probably will be. The Japs will be in the toughest places and naturally on the best ground.

"All my time in the Marines I have seen men bunch up and I have talked about this and make my N.C.O.s talk about this all the time. The men seem to fear separation.

"The Japs are man-monkeys, and they run around considerable. In order to compete with these man-monkeys from Japan, you got to be in excellent shape and you got to be tough. We can lick them and we are doing it all the time, Sir.

Sanitation—I Know it's Right

"I have seen some awful attempts at individual cooking. However, some of my men have got to the point where they can make jam tarts.

"Sanitation—*I know* it's right! To violate it causes billions of flies and sickness. Some lousy undisciplined recruits defecated in fox holes, which caused trouble in the dark. We learned that individual cans should be buried. Some of the recruits threw the empty cans in the creek. Then, I heard that the next battalion came along and went in swimming and cut their feet. When you occupy a position for several days in the tropics, the sanitation problem becomes tremendous. The young officers and N.C.O.s must get after this at the start and keep after it all the time."

Master Gunnery Sgt. R. M. Fowle.

Confidence in Each Other

Results of a conference with three 2nd Lieutenants and five old N.C.O.s.

"You gotta have confidence in each other. When signals to move forward are given, you must have confidence that the men next to you will move forward even if you cannot see them. We have that kind of confidence in this battalion.

"We have developed signals in our battalion which are not

recorded in any text book. I recommend that your troops do the same.

"One night when we had a position on a steep ridge, the Japs attacked up the ridge. We pulled the pins of hand grenades and let them roll down hill. Don't forget to count 'one Jap dead, two Japs dead,' before throwing the grenade. We had a Marine killed in this battalion because he forgot to count, and a Jap picked up the hand grenade and threw it back.

"We love the heavy machine-gun.

"The Thompson sub-machine-gun or carbine is needed, as they execute their attacks en masse. We understand the carbine will have more penetrating power than the Thompson.

"We have two American Indians we use as 'talkers' on the telephone or voice radio when we want to transmit secret or important messages.

"Don't forget the Japs make noise when they move too. They are not supermen.

"Be mean and kill 'em. Kill 'em dead."

Be Quiet, Listen and Look

"We have a lot of trouble in my platoon with water discipline. We also have trouble with men bunching up in order to talk to each other. They seem to do this even though it means death.

"We have learned to make reconnaissance before moving into an area. We scout for ambushes. We have learned to be quiet, listen and look. I sure like to see that artillery come down on an area before we move into it.

"The big problem which we have not solved completely yet to my mind is maintaining contact in the attack between units in this jungle, especially between battalions.

"It takes *guts* to go up on the Japanese position to throw grenades and to attack.

"This reconnaissance, which is so important, is also hard work because the Japs move their defensive positions.

"I was on my first patrol here, and we were moving up a dry stream bed. We saw three Japs come down the river bed out of the jungle. The one in front was carrying a white flag. We thought they were surrendering. When they got up to us, they dropped the white flag and then all three threw hand grenades. We killed two of these Japs, but one got away. Apparently they do not mind a sacrifice in order to get information. They are tricky bastards.

"The mortars are very effective here. An example: We were moving up a trail. We were stopped by machine gun fire. I withdrew the platoon and spread out off the trail, forming a skirmish line. I sent word back to the mortars to set up. They had to cut down some trees in order to set up properly. The OP man comes forward and gets the azimuth and paces off the range as best he can. Then the mortars open up."

2nd Lieut. D. A. Clark.

Analysis of the Enemy

"We feel that we have been successful. We have caused the enemy enormous losses in men. Our battle casualties to date exceed 3,500, of which about one-third have been killed in action.

"Most of the fighting here has been carried out at extremely close range and there has been as much throwing of hand grenades as in firing a weapon. *No previous report, or even comment, on our enemy and our fighting has been made.* For one thing, we do not want to appear boastful; for another, we have been literally so busy we have not had time to think things out.

"Concerning our enemy, several things are apparent. All of his efforts have been in the form of attacks on a narrow front at rather widely separated points. These were mass attacks, and although orders and operations maps captured have shown that they were to be simultaneous attacks, this was never the case. Our feeling is that his failure to estimate the terrain difficulties caused the lack of co-ordination. The result has been favourable to us, as it has permitted the shifting of our all too small reserves from one area to another.

"We believe that the enemy has dispersed his efforts and has therefore failed to make any gain at any one point. When given his choice, he operates exclusively at night. As I said before, he attacks on a very narrow front, practically *en masse*. This leads to many 'purple nights' when we watch longingly for sunrise. The result for him has been almost complete annihilation in every case. As far as we can determine, these various attacking groups are started out, and there are indications that they pass out of real control of their higher leaders. We have never seen anything to indicate that any effort has been reinforced after the initial push has been made.

Taken Practically No Prisoners

"The Japanese soldiers fight with a sort of fanaticism and never surrender. We have taken practically no prisoners. Officers about to be taken prisoner sometimes commit suicide. Perhaps of greatest assistance to us has been captured orders and maps. A great deal of information has been gotten from captured diaries. Our interpreters on the spot were able to get from captured orders information on which we have successfully operated at once. It causes me to want never to write another order.

"The Japanese try all of the tricks, make all of the noises, and infiltrate as many snipers as is reported they did in Bataan and Malay. These things have little effect on good troops who hold their positions, which they can do with safety and fight them when they come up. So far as I have been able to determine, though we have had hundreds of snipers in our position, only one man has been killed by a sniper. We usually get every one of them. Don't worry about them. They are ducks on the pond when daylight comes.

Otherwise he loses Control

"In their air attacks and in their ground operations, the Japanese appear to follow very definite patterns. Each attack appears to be the same. They are easily disconcerted by surprise, and if they fail to succeed in what is apparently the only way they know how to fight, they become ineffective. We have carefully avoided night attacks, making all of our offensive moves by day. Our officers feel that the Japs have placed so much stress on night fighting that they cannot or do not fight well at all in the daytime.

"Our officer casualties have been high. We have lost a number of company commanders and quite a few battalion commanders. We have managed to keep up our officer replacement by field promotions of selected non-commissioned officers who have proven themselves in battle."

Col. G. C. Thomas.

WAR

Enemy: Japan

ABCA 'War' Pamphlet No. 48, July 10th, 1943

Lines of Thought

1. This map makes a useful starting point.
   The dotted lines indicate Japan's progress up to December, 1941.
   The unbroken lines show the present position; simplified for blackboard reproduction.
2. This bulletin is divided into four parts:—
   i. The Broad Strategy.—As indicated by the Prime Minister in his recent speech to Congress in Washington.
   (See page 75.)
   ii. The Practical Difficulties of campaigning in the Far East, particularly our own troops' difficulties in Burma.
   (Page 78.)
   iii. A Successful Experiment.—Brigadier Wingate* describes

---

* Orde Wingate formed the 'Chindits' (lions) who employed hit-and-run guerrilla tactics behind the enemy lines in Burma. He died in a

the recent reconnaissance in force under his leadership.
(Page 81.)

iv. Situation Report.—Summary of what has happened in
the Far East during the last six months.
(Page 89.)

3. There can be no peace until the Japanese are beaten. Make
sure that your men realise this.

---

plane crash in 1944.

(1) _Mr. Churchill at Washington_

In ashes they must surely lie

Here are the references to the war against Japan made by the Prime Minister in his speech before Congress on May 19th, 1943.

"ONE after another, in swift succession, very heavy misfortunes fell upon us, and upon our allies, the Dutch, in the Pacific theatre. The Japanese have seized the lands and islands they so greedily coveted. The Philippines are enslaved, the lustrous, luxuriant regions of the Dutch East Indies have been overrun. In the Malay Peninsula and at Singapore we ourselves suffered the greatest military disaster, or, at any rate, the largest military disaster in British history.

All This and Much Else

"Mr. President, Mr. Speaker, all this has to be retrieved, and all this and much else has to be repaid. And here let me say: let no one suggest that we British have not at least as great an interest as the United States in the unflinching and relentless waging of war against Japan. But I am here to tell you that we will wage that war, side by side with you, in accordance with the best strategic employment of our forces while there is breath in our bodies and while blood flows in our veins.

"A notable part in the war against Japan must, of course, be played by the large armies and by the air and naval forces now marshalled by Great Britain on the eastern frontiers of India. In this quarter there lies one of the means of bringing aid to hard-pressed and long-tormented China. I regard the bringing of effective and immediate aid to China as one of the most urgent of our common tasks.

The Points That Arise

"It may not have escaped your attention that I have brought with me to this country and to this conference Field-Marshal Wavell and the other two Commanders-in-Chief from India. Now, they have not travelled all this way simply to concern themselves about improving the health and happiness of the Mikado of Japan. I thought it would be good that all concerned in this theatre should meet together and thrash out in friendly candour, heart to heart, all the points that arise, and there are many.

"You may be sure that if all that was necessary was for an order to be given to the great armies standing ready in India to march towards the Rising Sun and open the Burma Road, that order would be given this afternoon. The matter is, however, somewhat more complicated, and all the movement or infiltration of troops into the mountains and jungles to the north-west of India is very strictly governed by what you American military men call the science of logistics.

"But, Mr. President, I repudiate, and I am sure with your sympathy, the slightest suspicion that we can hold anything back that can be usefully employed, or that I and the Government I represent are not as resolute to employ every man, gun and aeroplane that can be used in this business, as we have proved ourselves ready to do in other theatres of the war.

The Ruin of Japan

"In our conference in January, 1942, between the President and myself, and between our high expert advisers, it was evident that, while the defeat of Japan would not mean the defeat of Germany, the defeat of Germany would infallibly mean the ruin of Japan.

"The realisation of this simple truth does not mean that both sides should not proceed together, and indeed the major part of the United States forces is now deployed on the Pacific front. In the broad division which we then made of our labours, in January,

1942, the United States undertook the main responsibility of prosecuting the war against Japan, and for aiding Australia and New Zealand to defend themselves against a Japanese invasion, which then seemed far more threatening than it does now.

"… It is all agreed between us that we should, at the earliest moment, similarly bring our joint air power to bear upon the military targets in the home lands of Japan. The cold-blooded execution of the United States airmen by the Japanese Government is a proof not only of their barbarism, but of the dread with which they regard this possibility.*

Begin the Process so Necessary

"It is the duty of all those who are charged with the direction of the war to overcome at the earliest moment the military, geographical and political difficulties, and begin the process so necessary and desirable of laying the cities and other military centres of Japan in ashes, for in ashes they must surely lie before peace comes back to the world.

"That this objective holds a high place in the present conference is obvious to thinking men, but no public discussion would be useful upon the methods or sequence of events which should be pursued in order to achieve it.

"Let me make it plain, however, that the British will participate in this air attack on Japan in harmonious accord with the major strategy of the war. That is our desire. And the cruelties of the Japanese armies will make our airmen all the more ready to share the perils and sufferings of their American comrades."

● *In his speech Mr. Churchill outlined the broad strategy and importance of the war in the Far East. Now consider a few of the difficulties of putting this strategy into effect.* ➜

---

* The 'Doolittle Raid' (or 'Tokyo Raid') was an American air strike on Toyo in April 1942. Eight of the flight crew who crashed in China were captured by the Japanese and three of them were later executed.

Only the snakes are neutral

THE work done by our troops in India has only been done with great difficulty. Most of them have had all the frustrations of static military life in this country, without the consolation of being in this country.

They had to prepare an unprepared country (with a 4,000 mile coastline) against invasion, after the fall of Singapore. And when the naval battles of Midway and the Coral Sea greatly reduced the seaborne threat to Ceylon and India, they had the fresh set of problems and difficulties involved in changing over to the offensive. For instance, many of the base and supply organisations which had been laboriously improvised to face the threat to Southern India and Ceylon were now facing the wrong way.

Ask, and it was Taken Away

The Army itself had to be differently equipped for its new task. To a large extent animals had to take the place of mechanisation. There was little help from outside India. Europe and the Middle East had to come first. India was not only asked for all kinds of help, but if she asked for something herself she usually had something taken away.

Training wasn't only hampered by lack of equipment. Burma is for the most part a land of jungle, tropically thick in the low country, and just as thick but cold at nights in the mountains.

It is very easy to say that all our troops in India should be trained for jungle fighting, but it isn't so easy to train them on the hot, sandy plains of India. Of course there are places where you can train them, and at these jungle training centres they are so being trained; but it isn't so easy to organise as it sounds.

Patrolling by Both Sides

But many of our troops have had more than adequate opportunities to learn jungle fighting. Some units have been up on the eastern frontier ever since the Japanese arrived in Burma.

The chief feature has been patrolling by both sides. The Japanese have been holding their front in the same way with no particular attempt to reduce the wide no man's land.

The main source of casualties has been malaria, which can reduce a unit's strength by 25 per cent. per month. The Bengal-Burma frontier is one of the worst malarial districts in the world. (For the Japanese as much as for us.)

No Routes Exist as Such

The whole problem of fighting in Burma is the Lines of Communication, and the difficulty of maintaining your troops in the forward areas.

No routes exist as such. We have to make them as we go, whereas the Japanese have existing lines of communication running north to south, from which to operate against us, up to Mandalay. Beyond that to the North-West things are just as difficult for them as for us.

As an example of the difficulties, there is no metalling on the Arakan Coast for road or aerodrome making. We have made a road running down the coast by shipping coal from Calcutta and Chittagong on to the coast, where mud is baked with the help of the coal into bricks. The bricks are then broken up and made into a road surface. Needless to say this is only a fair weather road, and involves many transhipments and ferries.

Up to Forty Feet

There are no established routes into Burma from India: there are only tracks capable of improvement. The improvements have to be strenuously maintained, otherwise the routes are grown over by the jungle once again.

There is the route followed by General Alexander in his withdrawal across the Chindwin towards Imphal. There is a route in the north which is just about passable by jeep. It has one 40-mile stretch which becomes a complete swamp in the height of the monsoon period. You have to go by boat.

There are rivers all over Burma and they mainly run from north to south, so in advancing from India you are going against the grain. In the monsoon, river levels will rise anything up to 40ft.

Because of these difficulties campaigning is normally only possible from November or December to May.

● *Of course, it is impossible to give anything like a complete picture of the problems involved. But having touched on some of them, we now come to the encouraging story of a successful attempt to cope with them, written by the Force Commander.* →

Intruder Mission

by Brigadier O. C. WINGATE, D.S.O.

THE object of the operation was experimental in character. It was to prove that columns composed of ordinary British and Indian troops could operate many hundreds of miles from their own bases in the midst of Japanese controlled territory. The principal factors which made this departure from recognised methods of warfare possible were aircraft and W.T.

As a result of these operations it may be held that the major propositions have been abundantly proved and that a weapon has been found which may well prove a counter to the obstinate, but unimaginative courage of the Japanese soldier and which will give scope to the military qualities which the British soldier still shares with his ancestors.

These qualities, hitherto in this war unsuspected by the world, are, firstly intelligence in action, i.e., originality in individual fighting, and lastly, on the morale side, great self-reliance and power to give of his best when the audience is smallest. Thus, while in the case of nearly every other nation a sense of drama and public approval is necessary to produce courage and effort, in the case of the British soldier he can be relied upon to excel himself even in jungle so thick that no one but himself can be a spectator of his actions.

An important point, therefore, to grasp is that the troops that carried out this enterprise were in no respect chosen for their fitness for this or any other type of warfare, but were simply the men who normally get drafted into the infantry during a great war. All the more remarkable, therefore, and worthy of admiration is their achievement.

Big Enough, yet Small Enough

It is undesirable to give the enemy exact details regarding the composition of a column designed for this type of operation. It is enough to say that the column is big enough to defend itself against anything the enemy is likely to be able to concentrate against it and at the same time small enough and mobile enough to slip through any net which the enemy attempts to draw round it.

In addition to these qualities it must possess the means of inflicting irreparable damage upon the enemy's vital centres, of communicating by wireless with its own Commander and with the air, and, finally, of forming a close and friendly contact with the inhabitants of the country traversed.

The force was concentrated at Imphal in early February. The march into Burma began at Manipur Road where the brigade detrained with some 3,000 men and 1,000 animals. On the march to Tamu exercises in co-operation with the R.A.F. were successfully carried out. At Imphal on February 8th, Field-Marshal Wavell, accompanied by U.S. generals, inspected the force, which then continued its march to Tamu. It was necessary at this stage to conceal the intention of the force from the enemy. The plan of deception was simple and was successful. The entire force crossed the Chindwin between February 15th and 18th. From there on the columns were in territory occupied by the Japanese.

More than 75 Breaks

The first objective of importance was the Myitkyina-Mandalay railway. This railway constituted the main Japanese line of communication from south to north and was supporting, at the time the columns broke into his territory, an offensive against us in the Sumprabum area. On March 3rd a column blew up the bridge on this railway between Shwebo and Wuntho, puzzling the Japanese by disappearing; to reappear later at the other side of the river.

On March 5th, 6th and 7th other columns blew bridges and

cliff sides on the railway line over a distance of 30 miles from the Meza Bridge to Wuntho in the Bonchaung gorge. In all the railway was broken in more than 75 places and ceased to function as such for the rest of the campaign.

By the time the first of these columns had crossed the Irrawaddy the enemy became alive to what was happening, and from then on made strenuous efforts both to prevent any more columns from crossing the river and to surround those that had crossed or were still on the west bank.

On March 17th the last of the columns crossed the Irrawaddy, proceeding southwards towards Mandalay-Lashio line of communications.

The threat to this line of communication, which is the main source of supply for Japanese forces operating against the Chinese, caused the enemy considerable alarm and altogether he was at this time disposing of up to ten times our number of troops in his endeavours to arrest our activities.

We Could Predict with Accuracy

In the course of operations we learned to know the Japanese enemy intimately. In fact, it would be true to say that, towards the end of the campaign, column commanders could predict with great accuracy the enemy's reaction to any given action on their part. This is by no means a universal or even ordinary condition in warfare. In fact, where you are able to predict the enemy's reaction accurately, other things being equal you should be able to defeat him.

Successful tactics and strategy are usually of a three-fold and not two-fold character, e.g., the first act is intended merely to provoke enemy action of which it is intended to take full advantage. It is the third stage, and not the first, in the operation that brings victory.

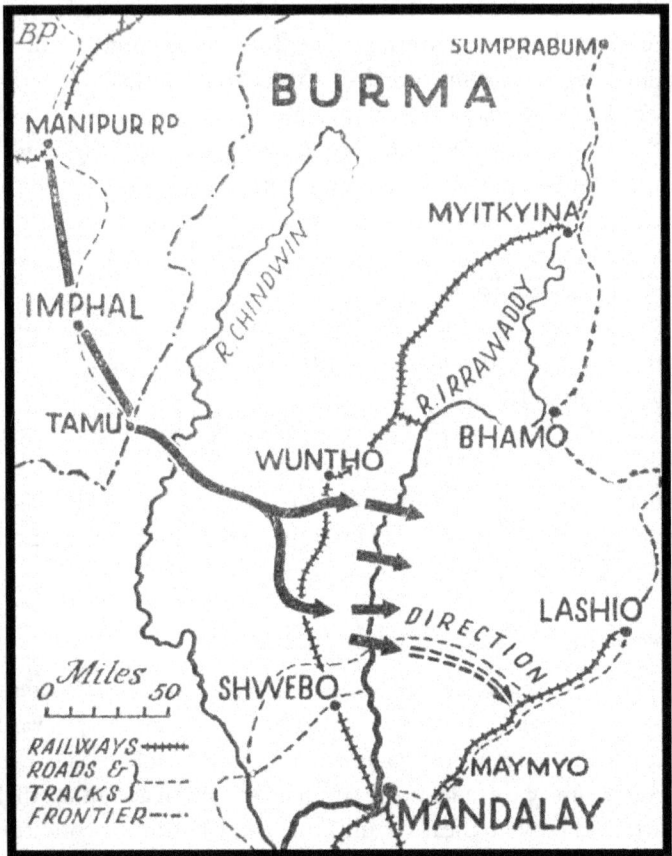

Think Fast, Private Moto

To descend to greater detail, the Japanese mind is slow but methodical. He is a reasoned, if humourless, student of war in all its phases. He has carefully thought out the answer to all ordinary problems. He has principles which he applies, not over-imaginatively, and he hates a leap in the dark to such an extent that he will do anything rather than make it.

When faced with a situation which he does not fully comprehend he will withdraw rather than chance his hand. On the other hand, when he feels he knows the intention and strength of his enemy he will fight with the greatest courage and determination to the last round and drop of his blood.

The answer is evidently never to let him know the intentions or strength of his enemy but always to present him with a situation which he does not thoroughly understand. The momentum of surprise, in other words, must be maintained against him. Now it happens that owing to our national characteristics we are capable of doing this while our modern education and Western outlook renders us incapable of his sombre and humourless self-immolation.

As soon as the Japanese obtained news that a column was in the neighbourhood of some L. of C. installation they would make feverish efforts to obtain news of its intention, strength and location. It was not normally possible for them to get accurate news under a good many hours, and this, normally, enabled the column to remove itself from the scene before the Japanese blow could be directed against it.

The inaccuracy, which is characteristic of the Axis in this war, led on numerous occasions to the Japanese delivering a heavy blow in the shape of mortar and automatic fire against bivouacs long evacuated by our own troops. Various methods were used both to mislead them and to discourage them from following up. It is not in the interests of the prosecution of the war that these methods should be discussed in detail.

Which He Could Not Analyse

Our own methods, as opposed to those of the Japanese, were always to present him with a new situation which he could not analyse; to ensure that our methods and intentions were unpredictable without losing our punch or power to injure.

It cannot be claimed that in the latter respect we were entirely successful, seeing that the inevitable absence of supporting operations by other troops left us open to a concentration of force against us which may be regarded as abnormal. This resulted in some columns becoming hunted and this again caused them to lose some of their power to hit back.

The dispersal procedure was originally practised by Robert the Bruce when warring against the English in the Lothians. The principle is briefly that when the column is hard pressed by a numerous enemy, a force sufficiently well commanded and with sufficiently high morale can break up into small component parts moving independently to a previously arranged rendezvous.

This method was tried out in order to evade the Jap net by most columns, and, on the whole, proved a success. The high qualities of junior leadership required were not always present, but they do exist in sufficient quantity amongst the Imperial Forces.

All officers and men who took part in this operation from start to finish marched not less than 750 miles, and the majority over 1,000 miles with, on the average, a good 60 lbs. on their backs.

This march was accomplished in 10 to 12 weeks. It lay not along roads or even tracks, but through the jungle and over the chaotic mass of formless hills that characterises the topography of Northern Burma.

Great and Probably Unsurpassed

It is true to say that on many occasions five to six miles made greater demands on the body than 50 miles of road marching, and that, on the average, 15 miles of this marching was equivalent to 50 along roads. The physical effort was, therefore, great and probably unsurpassed in recent military history.

As I expected, the prolonged effort demanded of the body prevented the appearance of diseases during the time of struggle but left the body in a weakened state at the end of the campaign. It must be remembered that the men who made these efforts were born and bred to be factory hands, dock hands, and to follow similar occupations in the close city atmosphere of Manchester and Liverpool.

Through Burma with Bernard Shaw

In many cases individual men with columns obtained special types of supplies by previous arrangement from the air. For example, a private in No. 5 Column received on four separate occasions a pair of special glasses from Calcutta, despatched regularly to the air base by his mother, who lived in that city. It is understood that he broke them at about this rate.

Several officers and men also had private arrangements whereby they would sometimes obtain a packet of some favourite tobacco or sometimes a book. The latter formed a most welcome addition to our slender amenities. For example, during the last week, when I was lying up to the east of the Irrawaddy, the appearance of the "Life of Bernard Shaw," by Hesketh Pearson, occupied us very pleasantly for many otherwise dull hours. As regards this, it is very necessary that all intelligent soldiers should provide themselves with some form of mental pabulum with which to refresh their minds.

Throughout the campaign, whenever supply dropping occurred we were furnished with recent papers and private mail. These were great comforts and made the unfortunate soldier in the wilds of Burma feel that he was in touch with the mighty war machine and not entirely cut off.

In spite of the one-sided nature of the communication, there is no doubt that such mail tended to raise morale and on future occasions return mail might be picked up by returning aircraft.

The Operation was a Success

No more should now be said about the possibilities of this new type of warfare, but it is again stressed that it is not similar either to the supply dropping that has been going on in the Pacific Islands or in the Chin Hills, nor does it resemble the resistance of Mihailovitch, or any other guerilla troops, whether maintained to some extent by air or not.

In its principal features the operation was a success. A considerable force entered Japanese occupied Burma through a front requiring to be held by an army corps, penetrated to a depth of 200 miles, smashed up a vital line of communications, arrested a Japanese threat to the North already developing, occupied many times its own number of Japanese troops, diverted the enemy's attention and confused his plans, and, while doing so, demonstrated a new method of warfare suited to the genius of the United Nations and one correspondingly difficult for the Axis to adopt.

● *But what has been happening in the Far East as a whole? The next section provides a general summary.* →

The Rising Sun at Noon

THE Japanese are now at the zenith of their power. They claim to be satisfied with their position and regard their "Co-prosperity Sphere" as permanently secured. Economically it is formidable. They have plenty of many things they were previously lacking.

In the last six months the Japanese have not extended the area of their conquests. On the contrary, they have lost Guadalcanal and its important airfield. Their hold on the western end of the Aleutian islands has been weakened and the prospect of war brought appreciably nearer to Japan itself. A large force in New Guinea has been wiped out and attempts on Port Moresby, at the gateway to Northern Australia, defeated. In Burma, the operations of the Wingate Force have shown us that the Japanese can be beaten in terrain in which 12 months ago we were in danger of thinking they were masters.

The most spectacular losses have been inflicted on them at sea, by air attacks on their convoys, and it is clear that safe movement of troops about the Pacific islands is impossible without air superiority, which the United Nations are far more likely to achieve than the Japanese.

South-west Pacific

Was Roughly as Follows

The position on the active fronts in the S.W. Pacific at the end of 1942 was roughly as follows. In Guadalcanal, on which the Americans had landed on August 6th, 1942, all Japanese attempts to wipe out the attacking force had failed. Their principal effort to

land reinforcements from the sea had been defeated in the naval battle fought off the coast between November 11-15th, when the best part of a division was lost and the convoy was wiped out.

Small reinforcements were sneaking in to the northern tip of the island, landed by destroyer and submarine, but, so far from turning the scales against the Americans, the Americans were gradually pushing the Japanese back, and the airfield, taken on the first landing, was now firmly held and in constant use.

In New Guinea, the Japanese assaults on Port Moresby, opposite the coast of Northern Australia, had been defeated. The last one, the overland attack from Gona and Buna, which in September was over the Owen Stanley Range and within 25 miles of Port Moresby, had been smashed and the remaining Japanese penned in along the northern coast of the island, partly by the Australians who had driven them back from Port Moresby, and partly by fresh American troops landed to the east of Buna on the northern coast itself. A feature of this campaign was the development of supply to forward areas by air alone.

Has Been Completely Retaken

Since the new year, Guadalcanal has been completely retaken. Organised resistance by the Japanese ceased early in February, and since that date activity in the Solomons was confined to the sea and air until the end of June.

In New Guinea, the Japanese started the year badly. A convoy from Rabaul to Lae, the next main base to the north-west of Buna, was caught at sea and on January 7-8th badly mauled by air attack. Two transports were sunk *en route* and two more in Lae harbour.

Meanwhile, Australian and American troops were pushing forward in the direction of Mubo and the Huon Gulf. The Japanese launched a big counter-attack against these in January. It was unsuccessful, although at one point it reached within 250 yards of one of our advanced landing fields.

On the failure of these attacks the Japanese withdrew further up the coast, some isolated garrisons being withdrawn by sea at night. Here again the Japanese were faced with supply problems, as our aircraft made the journey from Rabaul by sea increasingly costly. Another convoy was attacked early in March and heavily damaged.

At the end of June the position was that, on land, Papua had been cleared of the Japanese, and their troops in the Lae-Huon Gulf area of North-East New Guinea were being pressed by patrols from the south.

On the last day of the six months covered by this résumé it was reported that the Americans had landed on Rendova Island, in the New Georgia group of the Solomons, 160 miles north-west of Guadalcanal, and within five miles of the Japanese airfield of Munda. The following day it was announced that Viru Harbour, in New Georgia, had been occupied, constituting a further threat to Munda airfield which is 40 miles north-west of Viru overland. Landings had also been made on two groups of islands off the New Guinea coast and at Nassau Bay in New Guinea.

Burma

Easy Come, not so Easy Go

The operations in Burma under Brigadier Wingate are dealt with separately in this bulletin, and the remaining activity along this front can be quickly summarised. There has been constant patrol activity along the Assam-Burrna boundary, with no considerable changes in the area controlled by either one side or the other.

The only other campaign undertaken was a thrust down the west coast of Burma towards Akyab by British and Indian troops, with the object of securing an advanced air base. The attack began in December. By January 6th our troops had reached Donbaik, only some five miles from the tip of the Mayu peninsula and

some 20 miles from Akyab. The Japanese retained their hold on the west side of the Mayu River, at Rathedaung, and were in control of the estuary.

During January there was little but air activity, but by March the Japanese had assembled increased forces at Akyab, and were counter-attacking, both frontally on the Mayu front and by infiltration behind our positions from across the Mayu River.

They extended their hold at Rathedaung early in March and, although we held their frontal attacks at Donbaik, our supply lines were in jeopardy from their infiltrations.

By April we were compelled to withdraw to the line Buthidaung-Maungdaw at the head of the peninsula. On May 5th the Japanese cut the Buthidaung-Maungdaw road and compelled the evacuation of Buthidaung.

By the beginning of June the monsoons had started and put an end to the campaign. This is not an area in which any troops could be maintained during the rainy season, owing to disease and supply difficulties, and the Japanese finally withdrew a large number of their troops to the Akyab area for the remainder of the summer. Japanese casualties were estimated at more than 900 killed and more than 2,000 wounded.

The Aleutians

Frostbite Causes Most Casualties

The campaign in the Aleutians is marked by two features, the importance of their position and the difficulties imposed by their climate. The islands are mostly volcanic. They are continually shrouded with mist, the weather is cold, and rain alternates with sleet. Frostbite causes more casualties than enemy weapons.

The Japanese occupied Kiska, Attu and Agattu in June, 1942. The American counter-attack on Attu began on May 11th, 1943, with successful landings at Holtz Bay on the north-east of the island, and at Massacre Bay on the south-west. Attu is about 35 miles long and 12 broad; mountainous, with a surface of lava rock, shale and moss-covered bog. Stiff resistance followed the landings as the Americans penetrated further inland. The high ground behind Holtz Bay was cleared despite heavy counter-attacks, and on May 18th the Japanese withdrew on Chicagof Bay. By the 25th the defenders had been split into small pockets and within a week resistance was at an end. The Japanese garrison was about 2,000 men. The Americans counted 1,791 bodies. Only 11 prisoners were taken.

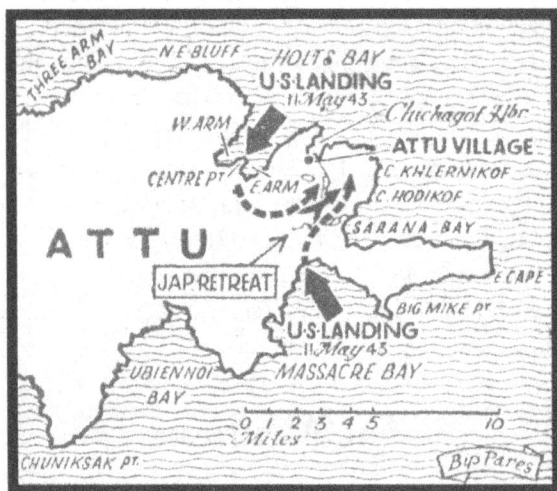

Air support on both sides was difficult owing to weather conditions. As at Guadalcanal, the American stroke was timed to capture the island at the moment when the Japanese were completing an airfield. Possession of Attu and its airfield will make supply to the Japanese troops on Kiska and Agattu more difficult. At the same time Attu is only 700 miles from Paramushiro, in the Japanese-held Kurile Islands.

China's War

The Japanese were Less Successful

Japanese activities in China during the first half of this year were confined to an expedition in force based on the Ichang area, some 400 miles down the Yangtze River from the Chinese capital at Chungking. South-east of Ichang are valuable rice-fields, and this raid was doubtless designed to interfere with the rice harvest. The strength of the Japanese force was in the neighbourhood of 60,000 to 70,000 men.

The Japanese crossed the river early in May and made some progress, particularly south of Ichang, but after about three weeks they withdrew from their advanced positions. They were followed closely by the Chinese and harassed by American bombers, and finally were unable to hold any of the ground that they had temporarily occupied, save one small bridgehead across the Yangtze River. The Japanese withdrawal was less methodical than usual, and the increased air strength of the United Nations in China made this raid less successful than those of other years.

Offensive action in China against the Japanese by the United Nations still remains a question of supply.

CURRENT AFFAIRS

How About Japan?

ABCA 'Current Affairs' Pamphlet No. 67, April 22nd, 1944

ENEMY JAPAN

A. 1st AGENDA: WHAT ARE THEY REALLY LIKE?

AT the present time our troops are engaged against the Japanese in at least three areas of Burma. We know what our men are like. What do we know of the men opposing them? Do they correspond at any point with the pre-war notions which some of us possessed of the Japanese as a nation of funny little men, who made excellent valets and invented ju-jitsu, who provided us with cheap toys and the stuffing for Christmas crackers, who spent their private lives, side by side with geisha girls, in the atmosphere of a Gilbert and Sullivan opera, and always addressed foreigners as "honourable sir"?

Is this an adequate picture of the small island nation, whose warriors, after an early series of the most sensational conquests, are now confronting our forces in the jungles and mountains of Upper Burma, on the frontiers of Assam?*

Clearly, this ABCA session requires a generous hors d'œuvre of facts. So pass the pamphlet round well in advance of the discussion, and open the discussion itself with a solid ration of information.

ARE WE TO REGARD THEM AS HUMAN?

Then, against the sentimental pre-war picture, set the opposite extreme: should we regard the Japanese as mere animals? Are they fundamentally so very different from us? (pp. 105-7). How

---

* *During this discussion, display the map of Burma on the front of ABCA Map Review, Number 37, and the reverse side of Map Review Number 29, "Far Eastern Battlefield."* [Note in orginal text]

much has early "conditioning" to do with their more unpleasant characteristics? (pp. 107-10). Does their religion support their view of themselves as a race apart? (pp. 111). How far has Western science influenced their lives? And have Western ideas really got across in Japan? (pp. 112-3).

B. 2nd AGENDA: WHY HAVE WE GOT TO BEAT THEM?

On this larger issue, John Morris has written:—

"The Far Eastern war is just as much our concern as the war in Europe. The principles for which we are fighting apply equally to the Far East; we cannot fight for justice in one half of the world and ignore it in the other. We are often reminded that this is a global war. We should also remember that a global peace is also necessary if we are not again to be drawn into war a few years after the present one is finished."

This is too big a subject for a single ABCA session, but it is a supremely important one.

ARE THESE GOOD REASONS?

Here is the opinion of another expert on this question:—

(i) *Two Kinds of World Order Cannot Exist Side by Side*

"The militarism of modern Japan, like that of Nazi Germany, is founded on a principle diametrically opposite to that on which the progressive civilization of Britain and the British Common-wealth is based, and it is not possible for the two kinds of world order to exist side by side, because the Nazi and Japanese systems are inherently expansionist, so that if either of them were left in possession of its conquests, the struggle would only have to be renewed later on. If Japan were allowed to hold her present gains and complete the conquest of China, her war machine would be enormously strengthened after a few years of peace and she would be a far greater menace to the world than she is to-day.

"Japan does not at present directly threaten the British Isles, as Germany does, but she endangers the Dominions of Australia and New Zealand, who have, without hesitation, come to our aid in both our wars with Germany and to whom we owe a debt of aid in return. The British Commonwealth as an association of free nations could not survive if Britain were to be unwilling to exert herself in defence of those who have so loyally helped her in the hour of need."

(ii) *Britain has Obligations towards India, Burma and Malaya*

"There is also the question of our obligations to India, Burma and Malaya. As British dependencies, these countries are not in the same category as the fully self-governing Dominions, and it is sometimes suggested that talk of defending them is only a cover for keeping an "imperialist" control over them, to which we have no more right than Japan has. But British policy has for a long time been to prepare these countries for self-government, and great progress towards this goal had already been achieved by 1941, whereas the Japanese in Korea and Formosa have not given the native peoples the slightest chance to develop self-governing institutions.

"The Japanese have indeed been ready to grant the form of independence in Burma and in the Philippines, but have kept a tight control on the puppet governments set up in those countries. Everywhere in the Far East there have been some politicians who have collaborated with the Japanese, like the quislings in Europe, but the Japanese have nowhere been accepted as liberators by the bulk of the population, because their reputation for cruelty and greed has gone ahead of them.

"Had the people of India had more confidence in Japan than in Britain, there would have been a real revolt in India in 1940 after the fall of France or in 1942 after the loss of Singapore, whereas, in fact, even the Congress Party was only able to produce some local riots by its call to rebellion. On all the evidence we have we can feel certain that the defeat of Japan really is in the interest of the other peoples of Asia and that it would be wrong for us to abandon them to Japanese rule."

(iii) *Britain has Economic Interests throughout the Far East*

"There is finally the question of British economic interest in the East. This is not the interest of a few companies with trading connections or investments there, but is a part of Britain's national interest in preserving the maximum freedom of international trade—a policy in which we are linked in common cause with the United States. The Japanese system aims at economic self-sufficiency, and wherever they go, the Japanese invaders monopolise trade for themselves. But Britain is the most dependent of all the great nations of the world on international trade, and it would mean disaster for Britain if the world were to be divided up into monopolists' spheres closed to the exports by which alone we can pay for the food and raw materials we need for our livelihood. Here again, though the issue is a material one, there is a principle at stake, and it is one which affects the British people as a whole."

Do members of your group think these cogent and convincing reasons? And have they any other reasons of their own?

C. 3rd AGENDA: "DON'T IMAGINE THEIR ARMY WILL CRACK"

You've now discussed what the Japanese nation is like. You've pooled your group's reasons why it is necessary to beat their armed forces into unconditional surrender. The third question is "How?" Before you can start to discuss that one, you must know something about the Japanese soldier and his training. Part II of John Morris's article gives you as much information on this subject as your group is likely to be able to digest at one sitting.

Q. AND A.*

Q. 1. What is the Japanese name for Japan, and what does it mean? (Answer: "Nippon," meaning "Sun Origin.")

Q. 2. How many people live in the islands of Japan—10 million, 50 million, 100 million, or more? (Answer: p. 105.)

Q. 3. What is the capital of Japan, and how many people live there? (Answer: Tokyo, nearly 7 million inhabitants.)

Q. 4. Which countries were conquered or otherwise brought into the Japanese "sphere" (a) before, (b) since Pearl Harbour? (Answer: p. 105.)

Q. 5. Are the Japanese illiterate barbarians? (Answer: pp. 108-10.)

Q. 6. Is Shinto the same as ancestor-worship? (Answer: pp. 110-1.)

Q. 7. Are their standards of physical fitness as high as in the British Army? (Answer: pp. 114-6.)

Q. 8. What is meant by the Greater East Asia Co-Prosperity Sphere? (Answer: pp. 119-20.)

Q. 9. What is meant by the following terms: (a) geisha girl; (b) genro; (c) harakiri; (d) ju-jitsu; (e) kimono; (f) samurai? (Answers: (a) a professional entertainer of men, not necessarily a prostitute; (b) elder statesmen, appointed as a check on the military. The last of them died in 1940; (c) literally, "belly-slashing," the Japanese form of honourable suicide; (d) invented by small men to deal with big men; (e) not a dressing-gown in Japan; (d) feudal retainers in old Japan.)

---

* *In administering the Quiz display the back of ABCA Map Review No. 25: "JAPAN."* [Note in original text]

How About Japan?

By JOHN MORRIS
Author of Traveller from Tokyo.

Part I

The Country and the People

1. Japan and Her Conquests

UNTIL the attack on Pearl Harbour in December, 1941, the Japanese Empire consisted of the islands of Japan proper (147,610 square miles), the island of Formosa (acquired in 1895), Korea (annexed in 1910), and Karafuto (the southern half of Sakhalin Island, separated from the Russian Maritime Province of Siberia by the Mamiya Straits. The northern half of Sakhalin Island is Russian). All these together added another 113,000 square miles to the Japanese Empire. The area of Manchuria (which is a Japanese possession in all but name) is 504,592 square miles, more than three times the size of Japan itself.

It is well to bear these facts in mind, for the Japanese excuses for their aggression are based largely on the claim that the country needs fields for emigration. Manchuria, which is capable of supporting an immense population, remains largely empty; and it is only by forcible means that the government is able even to stabilise the Japanese immigrant population of that country.

The Japanese leaders have in recent months referred to the total population of their own country as being one hundred million; seventy million is generally regarded as a more accurate estimate.

When Japan entered the war in December, 1941, she was already in possession of a large part of China. Since then she has conquered the whole of Malaya, all the Netherlands East Indies, the greater part of Burma, the Philippines, Borneo and innumerable islands, both large and small, in the South and South-West Pacific, and even the Andaman Islands in the Bay of Bengal, only a few hundred miles south of Calcutta. Both French Indo-China and Thai (Siam) are now Japanese in all but name. All these conquests were carried out in less than one year, and by a country that only 80 years ago was completely medieval and cut off from all contact with the outside world.

2. The Country Itself: Modern and Highly Efficient

It is important to realise that Japan is a modern and highly efficiently run country in the full Western sense; in some ways more efficient than Britain. The Japanese railway system, for instance, is more up-to-date than ours; not because the Japanese are more efficient as railway engineers than we, but because they introduced railway traction comparatively lately, so that most of their equipment is modern. Electricity, too, is more widely used in Japan than in Great Britain, the most remote country villages being supplied with current from one of the most efficient power systems in the world.

The country is extremely beautiful, and contains almost every variety of scenery and climate. It provides excellent sea bathing in summer, and in the winter it is possible to be ski-ing within a couple of hours of leaving Tokyo.

No country in the world has been so sentimentalised as Japan. It has, however, suited the Japanese to have their country described by foreign writers as an amiable paradise peopled by nit-wits with charming manners. Since the war another school of writers, going to the opposite extreme, has described the Japanese as ape-like barbarians, no more than sub-human, whose conception of co-operation with the West is to flood the markets of the world with cut-price bicycles and cheap contraceptives produced by means of the most appalling sweated labour. Neither of these points of view is correct; no people is wholly good or wholly bad; and the idea that the Japanese are somehow "different" from the rest of the world has resulted in a great deal of muddled thinking.

3. The People: Are They Human?

A special correspondent has recently pointed out in *The Times* that Australians who have had experience of fighting German and Italian troops look upon the Japanese as a sort of animal, "They cannot conceive," he notes, "that he is capable of the same human emotions which they themselves feel—fear, love or home-sickness. Some learn with surprise that the Japanese soldier can read and write, and are shocked if told that the standard of literacy is higher than in both Australia and the United States. The truth is that the Japanese soldier is a very human being and an unwilling exile, but his training, both in the army and in civil life, has been very different from that of the allies, and very much stricter." I should like to state that my own experience in Japan bears out the truth of this statement.

4. The Family is Everything …

In order to understand the fundamental difference in training between ourselves and the Japanese it will be necessary to consider their family and educational systems in some detail. It is during the school period that the chief "conditioning" of the Japanese people takes place.

In spite of Western influence and the modernisation of the country, the Japanese conception of the family remains largely feudal. It is important to note that in Japan the individual is considered of no importance; the family is everything. No important decision is ever made without a family consultation, and the family comprises not only a man, his wife and children, but all the senior relatives, and great deference is paid to the senior male members of this extended family.

The Japanese are extremely fond of children, and it is in the life of the child that the first great difference between the Japanese and ourselves can be discerned. In the West, children are for the most part brought up strictly; they are at any rate considerably restrained during their early years. When they begin to go to school they gradually acquire freedom; by the time they reach a university they are practically free to order their lives as they wish. In Japan the process is reversed. The young child is allowed to do exactly as it likes, particularly if it is a boy. It is most unusual for parents to check their children in any way. But as soon as the child starts to go to school the restraining process begins, and the first stages of what might be called "national conditioning" are introduced.

5. Education is Potentially Excellent

Japan has potentially one of the best educational systems in the world. Its outstanding merits are that it is both cheap and egalitarian, the schools and universities in Japan being open to all without regard to wealth or class.

A sharp distinction is made between government and private educational institutions. Nearly all schools up to the secondary grade are controlled by the government, the only exceptions being a few missionary and private foundations. To-day, however, the education provided in the latter in no way differs from that given in the government schools. About 90 per cent. of the youth of Japan receives its education, at any rate up to about the age of 16, in a government school.

Higher education is provided by the government in the Imperial universities, the one at Tokyo being the largest and best. There are in all six Imperial universities in Japan, and one each in Korea and Formosa, the total number of students being about

22,000, with a yearly graduation of some 7,000.

No one who has not taken his degree at one or other of the Imperial universities can hope to be employed by the government, and most students do in fact take up some form of government work. A government post is every boy's ambition. It means security; not for him alone, but also for his parents who, together with other relatives, are in many cases pinching and scraping in order to help him through his university years. This is a good example of one side of the working of the Japanese family system.

All teachers in Japanese government schools and universities are civil servants, as a result of which they cannot afford to express their private views, however liberal and humanitarian these may be; they must conform to the official government ethic.

Military training is compulsory in all Japanese schools and universities, including even the Academies of Art and Music. Every educational institution throughout the country has a number of army officers attached to it, the majority of them being on the active list. They are in theory subordinate to the principal of the school, but in present-day Japan no mere pedant dare oppose the wishes of the military. The result is that the syllabus is constantly being interfered with in order to make time for extra military training. It need hardly be said that the only interest the Japanese army has in education is to get it over as soon as possible in order to swell the flow of recruits. In order to do this, the holidays in all Japanese schools and universities have recently been curtailed so drastically as to constitute a terrible menace to the health of the rising generation. But the Japanese army is no longer in a position to consider long-term policy.

Education in Japan is compulsory up to the primary standard, that is up to about the age of 14, but as in all countries the tendency is gradually to raise the school-leaving age. The primary standard is roughly equivalent to that of an elementary school in Britain. The majority of recruits in the Japanese army will have received at least a primary education. After enlistment they will have received a further education designed to strengthen their belief in Japan's divine mission.

6. What are the Japanese Taught?

The Japanese are taught that their first *human* Emperor was one Jimmu Tenno, a great grandson of the grandson of Amaterasu, the Sun Goddess. Jimmu Tenno is believed to have ascended the throne in 660 B.C., and it is from this year that their era dates; thus, the year A.D. 1944 is the year 2604 in the Japanese era. However, it was not until about one thousand years after 660 B.C. that the Japanese began to keep records, as before this they had no written language.

The earliest Japanese histories are the *Kojiki* (Ancient Chronicles), A.D. 712, and the *Nihongi* (Record of Japan), A.D. 720. Both books are compilations of primitive creation legends and genealogies constructed to support the theory that the Emperor is directly descended from the gods and therefore himself divine. The conception of the Japanese people as divine comes from the idea that the Emperor is the father of one huge family which comprises the whole nation.

Japanese mythology is probably no more absurd than the mythology of any other country. The difference, and it is a great one, is that many Japanese, especially the peasants, take their mythology seriously, and it is true that it has been used by the militarists as the ethical justification for armed expansion.

The religion of Jimmu Tenno and his followers was probably a simple form of animism in which spiritual life was linked with nature. Many traces of such beliefs can still be found in present-day Japan.

Shinto, the official religion of modern Japan, was a much later invention. The word *Shinto* is a Japanese copy of two Chinese ideographs meaning simply "The Way of the Gods." In its original form it appears that Shinto was little different from ordinary Chinese ancestor worship; and certainly it is in this form that the ordinary Japanese is familiar with Shinto. Japanese children are taught to begin their day by standing before the family shrine (one of which is found in every Japanese home) and bowing with clasped hands and closed eyes to the memory of their departed relatives.

As the child grows older and goes to school this worship is gradually extended to include all the progenitors of the family, and finally of the nation and the Emperor. In the life of the individual Shinto is ancestor worship; in the life of the community it is Emperor worship.

7. Do They Believe in Their Divinity?

I should say that no intelligent Japanese really believes in the literal truth of his country's mythology. He looks upon it much as an intelligent Christian regards the Old Testament, as a mixture of fact and fancy. The same applies to the divinity of the Emperor; but certainly no Japanese would at the present time admit his disbelief in public. To do so would mean arrest and possibly imprisonment.

Nevertheless the myth of divinity has played an exceedingly important part in the expansion of nationalist feeling, and the Japanese militarists have cleverly exploited it to gain their ends. The myth has been built up by methods similar to those adopted by Goebbels for misleading the German people, also that employed by the manufacturers of soap and tooth paste; but the Japanese first thought of the idea. They do not necessarily believe the myth; but since they are never for one moment allowed to forget it, there comes a time when all but the intelligent and sceptical tacitly accept it. Indeed, economic necessity does not allow them to do otherwise; it is not possible in a country like Japan to hold views diametrically opposed to those of one's leaders.

8. Their Attitude to Foreign Ideas

It would be possible, I think, to divide the Japanese into three distinct classes, each of which represents not only an age group, but also a point of view. First, there is a group which comprises most of the youth of the country up to the age of 25 or so. The outstanding characteristic of this group is mental confusion. It should be remembered that this generation received its first education at a time when liberal thought was still comparatively popular in Japan. The higher education many of them are at present undergoing is based entirely upon occidental ideas, and the more intelligent of them see quite clearly that there is no real hope for their country until such time as it assimilates not only the material benefits which the western world has to offer, but also its social and political ideas. It should be noted, however, that in the past few years elementary education in Japan has become extremely nationalistic, and in spite of the paper shortage caused by the war, many of the standard text-books have been rewritten to give them a more national flavour. Subsequent classes of students are therefore likely to be very different psychologically from those of the present generation. It is in fact likely that the "re-education" of these classes may later prove as great a problem as will undoubtedly arise in post-war Germany.

The second group comprises all the men between roughly the ages of 25 and 45. Contained in this group are most of the violent reactionaries. Many of them have received a western education and are nationalistic almost to the point of insanity; they understand the necessity for a close study of the West, but only as a means of destroying it. I was always amazed at the speed and suddenness with which the first group changed to the second after entering upon a career. It was as striking as the psychological change that takes place in the young men of more primitive communities who have to undergo an initiation ceremony. The reason is, of course, largely economic. The youth of Japan is not alone in coming under such pressure, but in no other country, excepting perhaps Germany, is the pressure so ruthlessly applied.

After the middle forties another striking change takes place. There is a tendency to ignore foreign ideas altogether, and to return to the traditional Japanese way of living. The men of this group, unless they be army officers, are not particularly anti-foreign; it is simply that they seem to give up the struggle. They take to the kimono in place of the European clothes to which they have long been accustomed, and spend their leisure in purely Japanese pursuits; the practice of calligraphy, the study of Japanese art, literature, and so on. This last change is in many ways comparable with that which comes over many English people who as they approach old age begin to take an almost morbid interest in religion. It should be noted that at no time does the father relax his hold over his children; in fact, as he becomes older he expects to be obeyed even more implicitly.

Part II

The Japanese Army

1. The People Who Guide the Country's Policy

At the beginning of the Pacific war there was a tendency to underestimate the Japanese army; later on, possibly as a result of our early reverses, we were in danger of looking upon it as almost invincible. It is certainly not that; but it is undoubtedly one of the most highly trained and ruthless military machines the world has ever seen.

One of the reasons why we have hitherto underrated the military efficiency of the Japanese is that they themselves always made elaborate arrangements that we should. They are past-masters in trickery, and they have, on occasion, gone to what might be considered absurd lengths to deceive foreign observers into drawing wrong conclusions.

For a great many years the Japanese have been taking elaborate precautions to conceal their real military training. Certain areas of the country have been designated as defended zones or special military areas, and no unauthorised Japanese, let alone a foreigner, would dare to venture anywhere near them. The Japanese went to extraordinary lengths to deceive the outside world, and with some success apparently, for there is no doubt that everybody greatly underestimated their efficiency.

It is necessary, I think, to draw a distinction between the regular corps of officers and the rank and file of the Japanese army, many of whom are at least unwilling conscripts. It is the officers of the Japanese army who are ultimately responsible for the atrocities perpetrated in the name of the army; it is they who have given birth to the insane nationalism which will in the end be not only the cause of their own loss of political power, but also the ruination of their country. The most influential among them are not, as might be supposed, the higher commanders, but the comparatively junior officers, the senior captains, majors and young lieutenant-colonels. These are the people who nowadays guide their country's policy: the actual Government of Japan is little more than a puppet in their hands. It is no longer capable of resisting the demands of the Army. The Government of Japan has become a form of government by assassination, and no man who is in any way opposed to the Army's policy will now serve in it, unless he be willing to risk his life. Unfortunately, lack of civic courage is a marked Japanese characteristic, although there have been exceptions in the past.

2. The Japanese Private Soldier

In the war in the Pacific it is probable that the greatest problem the Allies have to face is the Japanese private soldier. It is on him, more than anything else, that Japan depends for the defence of the so-called "Co-Prosperity Sphere."

The Japanese army is recruited entirely by means of conscripts and these are divided into three classes. The first includes all those whose physique is sufficiently good to permit of their immediate enlistment upon reaching the age limit. The necessary medical examination takes place at about the age of 19, in many cases while the prospective recruit is still at school.

In the second category are those of slightly inferior physique. Up to the time I left Japan (August, 1942) these lads were not being called up until about one year after medical examination. This class is looked upon as the first reserve of the army, and in normal times those placed in it are not called upon to serve. They receive no training and merely remain as potential reserves until they pass the age limit. Before the war, very few conscripts were taken from the towns, the army being able to meet all its normal requirements by recruitment from the country districts.

The third class consists of all those who fail to pass the medical examination. Men in this category are normally exempt from all military obligations, but a few whom I knew personally were called up for further examination in 1942 and taken into the service. Some of them had reached the age of 30 and were, I should say, quite unfit for a life of active service.

Defective sight is not considered any bar to service, even in the navy. I have often seen sailors wearing spectacles, the very thick lenses of which showed them to be suffering from pronounced myopia. It is only comparatively recently that the British Army has accepted recruits whose vision needs correction. Behind this there lies, I believe, a regard for appearance, spectacles being held to give the face a pacific rather than a military aspect. A scientific friend of mine tells me, however, that these short-sighted persons are not congenitally deficient in the warlike spirit.

But long before the war Japanese prowess in all forms of sport and athletics (some of their best performers are extremely short-sighted) should have convinced us that the Anglo-Saxon dislike of spectacled soldiers was based merely on the ancient prejudice of the "spit and polish" school.

3. The Training of the Japanese Army

When a recruit joins the Japanese army the first thing he is taught is that he must look upon dying as a duty. This is impressed upon him constantly, not only in verbal exhortations, but by posters which are stuck up in every barrack room.

In the past few years quite a number of books have been written by Japanese soldiers describing their experiences in the China campaign. The authors, for the most part, are cripples, or men who have been otherwise incapacitated, but in spite of this they always open their books with a humble apology for being alive. Nor is this an empty formula; there is no doubt that the Japanese soldier who returns to enjoy civilian life really does feel that he has failed in his duty to the country. This feeling also accounts for the shame felt by the Japanese who are taken prisoner. Some foreign observers have derided this state of mind, but, in my opinion, wrongly, for in the individual soldier's willingness to die lies the strength of the Japanese army. The sentiment has often been described as fanaticism; but it equally deserves the name of bravery. We should be unwise to decry it or to refuse to recognise wherein the strength of our enemy lies.

A great deal of training is now carried on in public parks and other open spaces in Tokyo. Even the streets in crowded parts of the city are used at any time of the day or night for practising street-fighting. I frequently found myself held up for 15 or 20 minutes in the Tokyo equivalent of Whitehall while some manœuvre was in progress.

All manœuvres are carried out in double time, even when it is a question of moving the position of a heavy machine-gun from one place to another.

Route marches of 30 to 40 miles seem to be part of the training; and often they are ended with a half-mile double. I have been told that the Japanese soldier never falls out during a march, and certainly I myself have seen men returning from a long march obviously on the verge of collapse. Some were being dragged along by their comrades with ropes.

4. Recruits Knocked Unconscious by N.C.O.s

Judged by European standards, discipline is harsh. An open space outside one of the schools where I taught was used as a practice ground for artillery units, and on several occasions I saw recruits knocked unconscious by non-commissioned officers. This was done in the presence of higher ranks, so I can only suppose that such behaviour is customary.

The Japanese idea of discipline is based on fear; the soldier is taught not to think, but only to obey. This applies also to the corps of officers. Some of my friends who have had the opportunity to observe the army at close quarters have told me that Japanese regimental officers are exceedingly efficient so long as they are not called upon to deal with a situation for which no provision has been made in their official text-books. In novel situations they are apparently apt to lose their heads. It would seem that this weakness is known to the higher command, for there is little doubt that the Japanese army does not as a rule, undertake any offensive operations before having done the most elaborate rehearsing, during the course of which the smallest details are practised over and over again; nothing is left to chance.

The reader will perhaps find this difficult to believe in view of the great success obtained by the Japanese troops in their campaign in Malaya and Burma. These operations were often carried out in what had hitherto been thought of as impenetrable jungle, and the nature of the fighting was such as called for a high degree of individual initiative in junior officers. It should be remembered, however, that before they embarked upon these campaigns the units of the Japanese army which took part in them received specialised training in the jungles of Formosa, Hainan and French Indo-China.

5. Yet Generals Strap-hang While Soldiers Sit

Side by side with this harsh discipline there runs an odd strain of feeling of equality, which owes its existence to the fact that the professional officers of the Japanese army are not normally drawn from the higher social levels of society. I have frequently seen private soldiers occupying seats in buses and underground trains with generals (as numerous in Tokyo as nowadays in London) strap-hanging* beside them. The private would invariably stand up and salute the officer when he entered the train, but, having done this, would then resume his seat. Incidentally, in the Japanese army all soldiers are required to salute anyone who is their senior, including, of course, private soldiers of a grade superior to their own. The effect of this in a crowded place is that they seem never to cease saluting.

I should say that the training in general was much more rigorous than in any European army. My house in Tokyo was not far from one of the big military rifle-ranges, and even in peacetime I used frequently to hear shooting between two and three o'clock in the morning, and that even in winter with the rain coming down.

On first joining the service, recruits are treated with particular strictness. For the first few weeks they are not even allowed to write letters, and during their first six months of training they are confined to barracks. After this they are given one free day a month, usually a Sunday. All letters written from barracks are strictly censored, as, of course, is all incoming correspondence.

6. Why Hitherto Have They Been so Successful?

Many people have asked me what it is that makes the Japanese army so strong. Behind all more direct answers lies the basic fact that the Japanese are not afraid of death, and hold that there is

---

* Suspended straps were gripped by standing passengers in order to maintain their balance.

no greater honour than to die in battle. This makes it possible for the General Staff to risk what in other countries would be looked upon as appallingly heavy casualties. Even if the Japanese people were to discover that these were often unnecessarily high there would be no public outcry. In point of fact the people are kept in ignorance, the figures of casualties being never made public. There must come a time, of course, when a shortage of man-power begins to be felt; but that time is not yet.

Another question I am often asked is: Why have the Japanese had no real success against China, which lacks all modern equipment? Well, I think there is no doubt that the Japanese General Staff originally expected to finish the China war in a matter of months. It is now known that in the early stages of the campaign the Japanese did not employ either their best troops or their most modem weapons and equipment. When they discovered what they were up against they changed their plans; and for the last three years they have been using the China battlefront largely as a training ground on which to prepare for the present struggle against Britain and the United States— a struggle which was undoubtedly envisaged by Japan's military leaders long ago. What they failed to realise, however, was the degree to which the China war was to unify, arouse and inspire the Chinese people.* If they might have defeated China five years ago by putting forward their whole strength, the position has now been completely altered by the heroic stubbornness of the Chinese people with which they have been opposed.

7. They are Definitely Out for World-Conquest

What is the ultimate war aim of the Japanese army? They themselves describe it as the establishment of what is called the "Greater East Asia Co-Prosperity Sphere." It is difficult to find

---

* The Army Bureau of Current Affairs pamphlet No. 88 (*Chinese Prospect*), February 10th, 1945, provides background information on China and its position in the war.

out exactly what this high-sounding phrase really means. Many of my Japanese friends would say quite frankly that they did not know. My own opinion is that the ultimate aim of the army is quite definitely world-conquest. This may seem fantastic, but at the time I left Japan people were saying quite openly that if the Allies lost the European war, which at that time seemed not impossible, Germany would be Japan's next objective. In fact, I once heard it said quite seriously that the Japanese army put the nations of the world into three classes: fighting enemies, neutral enemies and friendly enemies, Japan's Axis partner forming the last class.

Speaking of the Japanese Army, General MacArthur had this to say of it: "The Japanese soldier is no easy enemy. He is a hard fighter, and one who fights courageously and intelligently. He gives no quarter. He asks no quarter. His tactics are to disperse along his enemy's lines rapidly in groups of never more than 1,000, and often half that number, and keep pushing in until he finds where his enemy is and then hit him. The Japanese are the greatest exploiters of inefficient and incompetent troops the world has ever seen. When the Jap contacts these sort of troops nothing can stop him."

8. The Way to Stop Them

"Never let the Jap attack you. Make it a fundamental rule, whatever your position might be, to be prepared for an attack. When the Japanese soldier has a co-ordinated plan of attack he works smoothly. When he is attacked—when he doesn't know what is coming—it isn't the same.

"The Japanese soldier has an extraordinary capacity to fight on to the end. He never stops. He believes that if he surrenders, his enemy will kill him, or that if the enemy doesn't kill him, he will be executed when he returns to Japan. He has no use for a quitter. Some soldiers have shown a tendency when they get into a tough spot or when it looks hopeless in front of them to fall back. That is the end."

Of one thing, at any rate, I am quite certain in my own mind: there is not the remotest chance of the Japanese Army cracking. It is an absolutely first-class fighting machine, and we should be fools to underestimate it. It will go on fighting until the bitter end. Not for one moment do I doubt that we can eventually destroy it, but for that the first condition is a proper realisation of the toughness of the job.

APPENDIX

A short list of recently published books recommended for further reading:—

Report from Tokyo. By Joseph C. Grew. (Hammond and Hammond, 1943. 2s. 6d.) An excellent summary of affairs leading to the outbreak of war, by the former American Ambassador in Japan.

How the Jap Army Fights. By members of the U.S. Army. (Penguin Special, 1943. 9d.) An admirable account of Japanese Army methods by four American officers who were attached to the Japanese Army in peacetime and have since fought against it in the Pacific.

New Guinea Diary. By George H. Johnston. (Gollancz, 1944. 10s. 6d.) Excellent first-hand account of the campaign in Papua by an Australian war correspondent.

Tokyo Record. By Otto Tolischus. (Hamish Hamilton, 1943. 12s. 6d.) Very readable account of Japanese politics during the last few years by the *New York Times* Tokyo correspondent.

Government by Assassination. By Hugh Byas. (Allen and Unwin, 1944. 10s. 6d.) The best account likely to be written of Japanese politics. Mr. Byas was *The Times* correspondent in Japan and lived in the country for 23 years.

Paper Houses. By William Plomer. (Penguin, 1943. 9d.) A book of short stories by an acute and sensitive observer. Strongly recommended as an introduction to Japanese social life.

Traveller from Tokyo. By John Morris. (Cresset Press, 1943. 10s. 6d.) By the author of this pamphlet, who left Japan in 1942.

CURRENT AFFAIRS

The Japanese Way

ABCA 'Current Affairs' Pamphlet No. 77, September 9th, 1944

THE OTHER ENEMY

THE article in this bulletin sketches the background of a people whom we mean to defeat, whom we hope to change, and with whom we will have to live in a world whose different parts are becoming more closely interrelated from year to year.

It has been written by a man who has lived among and studied the Japanese for many years. He discloses the sources from which so much savagery, dishonesty and insane ambition have flowed, suggests how these fierce currents might be canalised and gives the short answer to the question: "Why fight Japan?"

IT TOUCHES US ALL

In six words it is: "Because their aim is world domination." Nothing less.

This may seem a remote threat to people living on an island in Northern Europe, but it is closer to our cousins who came across the world from Australia and New Zealand to help us when we were in danger; to the Indians, who have the enemy on their frontiers; to the Americans, living on the other side of a navigable ocean, and with a memory of the names of Pearl Harbour, Bataan and Corregidor. And for the Chinese, for millions in the Pacific and Indian Oceans, for thousands of our own flesh and blood in prison camps, their designs have become a cruel reality.

So comprehensive a threat cannot leave us unmoved. And even on a cash-book basis—to come back to ourselves—Japanese economic imperialism meant smaller wage packets and queues at the Labour Exchange for some of our industries before the war.

The importance of this bulletin as a discussion subject is, therefore, not likely to be denied. But it is not, necessarily, an easy subject to take.

TWO LINES OF ATTACK

There are two possible approaches, either by a discussion based purely on the facts known to, and the opinions held by, the members of your group, or, if you are to get full value from this bulletin, by a more informative type of session, with the facts mainly enumerated, but partly elicited by you, and with the discussion following. For both, by the way, you should have a map, and should build up your points on a blackboard.

As an example of the first approach, you could discuss the general topic, "Why Fight Japan?" Subdivide your subject. Thus:

1. Why are we fighting Japan?
2. What would happen if we didn't?
3. Summing up.

A PATCHWORK QUILT

If you are going to attempt an informative type of ABCA session, try not to produce a lecture, but draw in the members of your group with question and answer. This, you may think, is not very easy. Few people know anything at all about the Japanese. But that is not quite true. From most groups you could move from the known to the unknown by eliciting such scraps as: The Mikado, Geisha Girls, ju-jitsu, dumping cheap goods, aggression, brutality, Hara-Kiri, a disposition (if we are to believe the newspaper cartoonists) to call one another "honourable sir," earthquakes, fanaticism, cheap toys, Christmas crackers and so on.

Even such uncorrelated bits and pieces as these can be used to build up the pattern of a country with an Emperor who is supposed to be a god, with a special attitude towards women, a formalised standard of behaviour, an industrious, resourceful, partly-industrialised and expansionist people, who do not believe that they are like other men.

SOME TIPS ON HOW TO DO IT

Here are some notes on this type of discussion, which have been drawn up at the ABCA College at Harlech:—

"The Informative ABCA should set out:—

"1. To provide or elicit information.

"2. To stimulate discussion leading to the formation of responsible opinion.

"Instructing the group in the factual basis of the topic may be done by a brief introductory talk, or more slowly in discussion form by question and answer.

"As a method of instruction group discussion is slow but effective; therefore selection of material is important. As a method of education demanding the active participation of the group, it is usually far more effective than a discourse, in making men think, and arousing their interest.

"The period should be planned as a whole. If a talk is to be given the officer should not follow it by saying 'Now who's going to open the discussion?' Rather discussion should grow easily and naturally out of the talk. The use of question and answer method helps to link talk and discussion."

ALL PART OF THE ABCA SERVICE

For other material on Japan, refer to: *Current Affairs*, Nos. 5, 13, 24, 43, 67, and *War*, Nos. 37, 48.*

A forthcoming issue of *ABCA Map Review* will have one side of the sheet devoted to a pictorial survey of the war in the Pacific.

Starting at the end of September the ABCA Play Company will be touring with a dramatised version of the material in this bulletin.

---

* This publication includes material from ABCA *War*, Nos.14, 24, 37, 41, 48, 85, 89, 96, and *Current Affairs*, Nos. 67, 77, 86, A99.

The Japanese Way

By "WILLIAM ADAMS"

1. Not as Other Men

I. They Live in Isolation

THE geographical situation of Japan has often been compared to that of Great Britain. The parallel is in some ways close, since both countries consist of islands off continents, and the continents off which they lie have been main centres of civilisation. But there is a significant difference: Japan is more isolated. The Straits of Tsushima, which separate Japan from the mainland, are eight times as wide as the Straits of Dover; further, on the other side of these straits lies Korea, itself an isolated peninsula off the Asiatic coast. The parallel would therefore be more exact if Great Britain lay 160 miles off the coast of Scandinavia, rather than 20 miles from France, so long the centre of European activity. This physical isolation of Japan has had a considerable effect upon the mentality of the inhabitants of the islands and lies behind much of what is strange and difficult to understand.

2. Japan Means "Sun Origin"

The Japanese call their country *Nihon* or *Nippon,* meaning "Sun Origin," a name given to the islands by the Chinese, in whose language it is pronounced *Jih-pen,* which in turn gave rise to "Japan" in English. Japan proper consists of four main islands: *Honshu* (meaning "mainland"), *Shikoku, Kyushu* (the southern island) and *Hokkaido* (the northern island). The winter climate is somewhat colder than that of Great Britain, a fleeting and beau-

tiful spring ending in a season of rain (end of May to beginning
of July), a hot summer and a long and fine autumn. The islands
are volcanic; they are subject to almost incessant tremors and to
periodic "natural disasters," such as tidal waves and typhoons,
which cause havoc on a wide scale. Hot springs abound and bathing in them is a national relaxation. The islands are mountainous and thickly wooded; they are of great natural beauty, which
is keenly appreciated by their inhabitants. Every square inch of
land is cultivated in some form or other; the precipitous sides of
mountains are skilfully planted with trees. In no country in the
world is the hand of man so evident everywhere. The sea, warmed
by a convenient current, teems with fish; the climate favours the
cultivation of rice, tea and all manner of fruits.

3. Cities are Large

The principal cities of Japan are on Honshu: *Tokyo,* the capital
since 1868 (the name means "eastern capital") is the main city
of "eastern Japan" and now has seven million inhabitants. *Osaka,*
the industrial capital, with three and a half million inhabitants,
and *Kyoto,* the capital of Japan from 808 till 1868 and the artistic
centre of the country, are in "western Japan." *Nagoya* with one and
a quarter million inhabitants has grown rapidly of late and is the
great industrial metropolis of "central Japan." All these cities are
on the Pacific side of the island and all have ancient traditions.

In more recent times *Yokohama,* the deep water harbour of
Tokyo, and *Kobe,* which performs a similar function for Osaka,
have achieved great importance; they are the centres of European
residents in Japan. *Nagasaki** in Kyushu is an ancient port and for
two centuries was Japan's sole window on to the rest of the world;
the Dutch were allowed to maintain a small trading station on an

---

* Eleven months after the original publication of this pamphlet,
Nagasaki was, of course, devastated by an American atomic bomb (9th
August 1945) which, combined with the bombing of Hiroshima three
days earlier, effectively brought the war with Japan to an end.

island in its harbour, and through the Dutch the Japanese knew something of world events. More recently still a group of four manufacturing towns on the Straits of Shimonoseki, separating Honshu from Kyushu, have grown in importance: *Shimonoseki* on the Honshu side and *Moji, Kokura* and *Yawata* on the Kyushu side (Shimonoseki and Moji have recently been joined by an under-sea tunnel). The creators of these cities now merit attention.

4. The Japanese Race is Distinct

The origins of the Japanese race are still the subject of dispute among scholars, but roughly speaking the Japanese are a mixture of South Sea Island stock and Mongol stock from Southern China. When the migrations of these people to Japan took place is uncertain; but they happened so long ago that, certainly by the second century A.D., the Japanese were a more or less homogeneous race, speaking their peculiar language.

The original inhabitants of the Japanese islands were of Indo-Caucasian stock; they are known as Ainu. They were pushed northwards into *Hokkaido,* the northern island of Japan, by the present Japanese, much as the Anglo-Saxon invaders pushed the Celtic inhabitants of Great Britain into Wales. A few remnants of them still inhabit the Hokkaido; they are remarkable chiefly for their hairiness and for their habit of tattooing moustaches on to the upper lips of their women.

5. They Have a Long History

The Japanese have had a long history, although written records date only from the eighth century A.D., some time before which they adopted Chinese characters to write their own very dissimilar language.

For a thousand years Japan formed part of Chinese civilisation and represented a variation on the Chinese theme. It is often asserted that the Japanese are mere copyists: this is not strictly true. A traveller from the Far East visiting Europe and arriving in England from the continent might well be pardoned for exclaiming "But they got it all from Europe!" The traveller would in a superficial sense be perfectly right: all Europe has grown great on imitation; it is, though, the subtle variations introduced by each nation on the common theme that are of real importance. The same is true of China and Japan.

6. They are Bad Linguists

Before the adoption of Chinese civilisation, the Japanese had no writing; they attempted the extremely difficult task of fitting Chinese "characters" to their language. If the writing of Japanese verges on the Surrealist, its pronunciation presents few difficulties, being not dissimilar to Italian. It is therefore the more remarkable that the Japanese are without exception the world's worst linguists; this disability adds to their physical isolation from the rest of the world and contributes to their sense of "not being as other men are."

II. How They Live

1. Accent on Loyalty, with a Difference

The Japanese conceive of their state as a pyramid, at the apex of which is their Emperor. The pyramid is held together by loyalty, and loyalty is the chief moral element employed in its construction; the accent, however, is always on loyalty to a superior rather than to an inferior or an equal (thus a Japanese would consider himself morally justified in loaning his wife into prostitution in order to obtain money for a superior). It follows that anything for which loyalty can be construed as the motive tends to be condoned in Japan.

2. The Family is All-important

The family in Japan is a miniature pyramid, which forms, as it were, the stones from which the main pyramid of the Japanese race is built. The individual is not considered as an entity in himself, but in relation to his family. Each family has its head, who exercises considerable influence over all the affairs of the family and who is responsible for their well-being. The Japanese, therefore, thinks of himself as a unit in a family rather than as an individual. He feels most keenly his responsibilities towards the rest of the family. He has little money to spend for himself; it must be spent in the interests of the family. This has its good side, since, under such a system, workhouses are unknown; rich relatives are bound to support indigent members of the family.

The family arranges marriages. This is usually done through a "go-between," generally an intimate friend, although professional "go-betweens" exist. The "go-between" finds a suitable wife or husband as the case may be, and is in a sense responsible for the couple, in so far as marital quarrels would be brought before him, and he would attempt to smooth them out.

3. Appearances Must be Kept Up

The "go-between" is an example of the typically Japanese institution of the middle-man. No quarrelling, no business deals are done direct; they are done indirectly through an agreed middle-man. By this method, the Japanese feel, embarrassment is spared to both parties; refusal becomes easy. Both sides are able to maintain their dignity and look their appropriate part—for looking the appropriate part plays a major role in Japanese life. These institutions are known to the "old Far Eastern hand" under the name of "face"; this term has unfortunate connections with "blimpery," and attributing all troubles to "face" undoubtedly cloaks more often than not an inability to reason out the problems; nevertheless, "appearances" to the Japanese, as to the Victorian middle-class, are almost as dear as life and the utmost sacrifices are made to "keep them up."

Indirectness therefore is the rule of life in Japan; hints are skilfully conveyed and instantly perceived, ambiguity an art as cultivated as clarity in France (indeed the Japanese Education Minister recently declared that "the Japanese language, unlike European languages, is not a vehicle for the clear expression of thought"). Alas! ambiguity and hints are not for international usage, and the subtle devices of Japanese social behaviour not for export, hence the snags and pitfalls so familiar to those who have had official dealings with the Japanese.

4. Women Observe the Three Obediences

The position of women in the family unit is an invidious one. They are subjected to "the three obediences": in youth obedience to the father, in middle age to the husband, and in widowhood to the eldest son in old age. Women may not own property outright. They are in all things subservient to their husbands; they would never retire before their husband came home, but sit up, wait for him and greet him bowing smilingly to the floor. Japan is therefore very much a male world in which men have everything their own way: small wonder that the Japanese male is fond of saying that to have the best of everything one should have a European house, Chinese cooking and a Japanese wife.

It is, however, only fair to add that Japanese women do have complete control in their own sphere. They run the house, look after the children and, while they do not often, except in the case of "modern" couples, go out with their husbands, they do go out and enjoy themselves with their own kind. The Japanese woman has a certain air of stability given her by the lack of fear of competition; that is to say that the go-between chooses a woman for her sterling qualities, not for her looks. Further, while most well-to-do Japanese would not hesitate to run after a pretty face or engage a Geisha as a mistress, the unlucky wife at least knows that, provided she has a child, her husband will not marry her rival and thus displace her. The Japanese married woman in consequence has an air of resigned serenity which is not without its attraction.

5. Most Japanese Work on the Land

The majority of the Japanese nation still work on the soil, and agricultural methods in Japan are not as modern as they might be, owing chiefly to the small scale of the individual holdings, which militates against the use of machinery indispensable in wide open spaces. Co-operative methods are employed, groups of five households coming together at certain seasons of the year to help one another with the planting out of the rice or the repair of paths and bridges.

Every inch of soil in Japan is cultivated in some manner or other. Rice is the staple crop except in the far north, and rice terraces climb up the mountain sides as far as is practicable and cover all the level ground; the strips between the rice fields are used for the cultivation of beans, much used in Japanese cooking. Ground unsuitable for the growing of rice, owing to lack of water or too great slope, is given over to vegetables, barley, giant radish, millet, wheat or the growing of mulberry canes for silk worms. The rearing of silk worms is the chief "cash crop" of the Japanese farmer; Japan produced 80 per cent. of the world's raw silk. The major part of the silk crop was exported to the United States.

In recent years Japan has specialised in the growing of all manner of fruits. These are grown in the most scientific manner possible, the peach orchards being models of skilful planning and pruning. They even manage to grow strawberries on concrete terraces facing south, so that they ripen in mid-winter. The catching of fish occupies the coastal villages, fish being a major article of food in Japan.

III. The Birth of this Modern State

1. Japan Came Out of Seclusion

The Japanese reorganised their country after the so-called restoration of the Emperor in 1868, when, owing largely to the forcible impact of the West—in the person of the American Commodore Perry, who appeared in 1853 and 1854—they opened their country to normal intercourse with the rest of the world, withdrew their Emperor from seclusion in Kyoto and placed him at the apex of the national pyramid.

The period of seclusion from 1637 to 1868 had further accentuated those Japanese tendencies to consider themselves "not as other men," to which their geographic isolation made them anyhow subject. After the restoration of the Emperor in 1868 the feudal or military nobility (*Daimyo*) were forced to abandon their privileges in exchange for monetary compensation and the country was divided into prefectures in the French way.

2. The Emperor Granted a Constitution ...

Under the Japanese system, provincial government is largely in the hands of the local inhabitants. The various district headmen, are appointed among the villagers themselves on a rotating principle, but school teachers, prefects of provinces, and now Shinto priests, are controlled by the central authority in Tokyo, where there is an immense and cumbersome bureaucracy. At the same time the Japanese set up a parliamentary system and the Emperor granted a constitution—looked upon by the Japanese as a gift from the divine Emperor to his people and thus inviolate—based upon that of contemporary Prussia. Prince Ito, a remarkable statesman who did much to guide Japan during her difficult years of transition, shaped the constitution and parliamentary system. The Japanese Diet, or parliament, has two houses: the Upper House being restricted to nobility and to worthy persons, to whom life membership is given; and the Lower Chamber, which is elected in the familiar manner.

3. But the High Command Dominated Parliament

The Japanese parliamentary system had certain inherent weaknesses from the start. For instance, the Army and Navy Ministers had the right of direct access to the Emperor, the nominal source of all power, which was accorded also only to the Prime Minister. Further, the Cabinet in Japan has to resign unless it is complete. The Army and Navy Ministers are by custom officers on active service and therefore at the beck and call of the High Command. The High Command, by withdrawing the Army or Navy Ministers, or by refusing to provide one for a Cabinet in the making, can either cause the Government to resign or frustrate its formation. Thus the Japanese High Command has come to play a predominant rôle in Japanese politics.

This is in a sense no new development, since Japan was ruled for centuries by Generalissimi, whose government was indeed known in Japan as the military government. Perhaps to offset this development, Prince Ito introduced the system of "Elder Statesmen," who acted as it were as a buffer between the divine Emperor, who could do no wrong, and the outside world. They exerted a wise and moderating influence until their numbers dwindled; Prince Saionji, the last of them, died in 1940.

4. "The Way of the Gods" was not Darwin's

The primitive superstitions of the Japanese included belief in the divine origin of the Japanese race and in the divine ancestry of the Imperial Family. Chinese civilisation with its accompanying Buddhism largely overlaid such notions for centuries and Buddhism until 1868 was the official religion of Japan. The primitive tribal beliefs of the Japanese were given the name of

Shinto, or the "Way of the Gods," as opposed to the Way of Buddha. Buddhism, however, largely engulfed Shinto: Shinto divinities were given Buddhist rank and received into the hospitable Buddhist pantheon. A mixture of the two arose, and it must be confessed that in the popular mind the mixture still exists.

With the restoration of the Emperor in 1868 came the restoration of *Shinto* and its extrication from Buddhism: Buddhism was itself for a time proscribed. As the Japanese achieved successes these were said to be due to the restoration of the Emperor and to his august virtue. Further, a sense of inferiority *vis-à-vis* the western world, which also led the Japanese to feel that they are not as other men are, encouraged them to compensate themselves by bolstering up the notion that at any rate they had a divine Emperor, and that, while Darwin taught the western world that its inhabitants were descended from monkeys, *they* were descended from the Sun-Goddess!

5. Success Bred Self-Satisfaction

In 1895 Japan defeated China, the ancient source of her civilisation. In 1905 Japan defeated Russia, one of the Great Powers of the west. After these events the feeling of inferiority turned to one of vast self-satisfaction. The Japanese felt that they were not as other men are, but that they were a great deal better. This further stimulated belief in *Shinto,* in the unique nature of the Japanese race, constitution and ruler; so that with every success which Japan achieved, Emperor-worship, self-worship and state-worship became stronger and stronger. In 1910 Japan annexed Korea, in 1918 Japan emerged on the victorious side from the last world war, in 1932 she virtually took over Manchuria … With each success the power of Shinto, the state ideology increased.

In 1940, with singular perspicacity, the Japanese declared that State Shinto was not a religion, by which, however, they were not slow to proclaim that they meant that it was "the religion of religions" and above all others; at the same time they recognised

Buddhism, Christianity (about 300,000 Japanese were Christians) and Islam simply as religions, which were placed under the department of education for their better regimentation. State Shinto being officially not a religion, it has been easy for the Japanese government to enforce attendance at its ceremonies. In September, 1943, a Japanese could write: "When we set our heart on the State, without borrowing the assistance of any high-sounding religion, we can rise above self," and could go on to observe that merely to believe in Christ or keep the law of Buddha were both "nothing more than theoretical fancies."

6. Failure is "Contrary to the Emperor's Will"

For a brief period after the last war, owing no doubt to the success of democratic institutions in defeating authoritarian Germany, Japanese statesmen did appear to try to make democracy work in Japan. The Washington Conference of 1922, however, saw the end of the Anglo-Japanese Alliance, which had given great satisfaction to the Japanese people. It saw also the signing by Japan of the naval ratio treaty, limiting the Japanese fleet. These were both sources of indignation to the Japanese people, by whom they were looked upon as failures. Now, since the Emperor of Japan is divine, he cannot fail. Any failure on the part of Japanese arms or statesmanship is therefore regarded as being "contrary to the will of the Emperor."

That which succeeds, on the other hand, is thought to be following the will of the Emperor. The Japanese "liberals" were thought to have failed and therefore when, in 1931, the Japanese military, without apparently the instructions of the Japanese Government, embarked upon their adventure in Manchuria, and when, in 1932, they had succeeded in occupying the three eastern provinces of China, they were able to say to the Japanese people: "we have succeeded, we are carrying out the will of the Emperor. The 'liberals' and plutocrats think only about feathering their own nests; we are carrying out the will of the Emperor, promoting his greater glory and that of the Japanese race."

7. The Military Carry On the Ascetic Tradition

This doctrine, together with the advantages which the Constitution gave the military, combined to make them extremely popular and to enable them to control the destiny of the country from 1932 onwards. Their control is based upon their contention of following the will of the Emperor. Loyalty, it has been said, is the cement which keeps the Japanese pyramid together. They pose as the foremost champions of loyalty. Further they pose as carrying on the ascetic traditions of the *Samurai,* the feudal retainers who would lay down everything for their lords. They have shown themselves only too willing to take their own lives to demonstrate the purity of their motives. To commit suicide is always honourable; it demonstrates infallibly "sincerity." No persons not willing to sacrifice themselves command whole-hearted respect in Japan. Almost by definition the "liberals" did not hold with *harakiri* (literally "belly-cutting"); the military therefore could always command public respect by resorting to it.

IV. The Urge to Expand

1. They Are Self-Supporting in Food

From the above it will have become apparent that the Japanese urge to expand is not merely an economic matter. Japanese State-Race-and-Emperor-worship provides the impetus to expand, but naturally Japanese expansion is also occasioned by material motives. The Japanese population has more than doubled itself since the opening of Japan to intercourse with the rest of the world in 1868 and it continues to expand. Its expansion, however, has never been as rapid as that of Great Britain in the 19th century. During the years of seclusion, Japan practised infanticide which kept the population at a steady level. This practice was discouraged after the opening of the country. Only a relatively small portion of the land of Japan is cultivable. Nevertheless, the Japanese are still self-supporting in food.

2. Industry is Concentrated in a Few Hands

Under the old régime in Japan the noble, the peasant and the merchant were regarded as being in that order of importance. However, after the opening of the country to intercourse with the rest of the world, the Japanese developed industry on the Western model. Economic power in Japan very soon became concentrated into a few hands. Industry was therefore early integrated in Japan, thereby greatly facilitating its development. At the present time the combines Mitsui, Mitsubishi, Sumitomo, Okura and Yasuda control over 80 per cent. of Japanese trade and industry.

3. Cotton Had to be Imported

The two major industries of Japan came to be the cultivation of silk, of which she produced 80 per cent. of the world's supply, and the export of cotton piece goods. The Japanese farmer cultivated silk as a cash crop and the raw silk was exported in vast quantities particularly to the United States. Practically no cotton, however, is grown in Japan and therefore the Japanese were obliged to import the raw cotton, principally from the United States, but also from India and, to a small extent, from Egypt and North China. The cotton industry, which became after the last war the major industry of Japan, was largely stimulated by the relative inactivity of Lancashire during the war. Next in importance to the silk and cotton industries are pottery and toy-making. These have achieved a high degree of development in Japan and were exported all over the world.

4. Heavy Industries Were Built for Armaments

Soon after the opening of the country the Japanese set up the

Imperial Steel Works at Yawata and encouraged the building up of heavy industry largely for armament purposes. Shipbuilding, to begin with under British tutelage, was greatly encouraged and shipyards on a large scale are to be found at Kobe, Osaka and Nagasaki. The Japanese merchant marine gradually grew to be one of the largest in the world in size.

While, however, the Japanese developed an integrated industry on a large scale, they contrived to keep the wages of the majority of the population on an agricultural scale. This enabled them to compete very easily with western nations with a so-called higher standard of living.

5. The Quest for Strategic Security

The prosperity of Japan depended very largely on her export trade, but the Japanese military were long anxious to achieve "strategic security." They were not content to obtain raw materials from abroad as in the case of cotton, but they wished themselves to own the sources of supply and thereby frustrate the possibility of blockade, which has always appeared as a bogy to the Japanese. In order to justify the acquisition of strategic security, the theme of Lebensraum* was as greatly fostered as by the Germans and for similar reasons.

6. Japs Do Not Like Emigrating

The Japanese have never tried to populate fully their own Northern Island of Hokkaido. Even since the conquest of Manchuria the Japanese Government has had the greatest difficulty in inducing Japanese to migrate to Manchuria, and what success has been achieved has been on a military basis. The Japanese, in fact, do not like emigrating. The only occasions on which they have emigrated with success have been to countries where, by their family system of sharing-profits, they have been able to undercut

---

* Literally, 'living room'.

local competitors by trading on an uneconomic basis. This they did with success in California and, to a certain extent, in Brazil.

As long as the islands of Japan are able to feed their population it can hardly be argued that pressure of population drives them abroad. The quest for strategic security has since caused the Japanese to wreck their two major industries; they now have no markets for their silk, and their cotton piece-goods are restricted to what meagre amount of cotton they are able to make the inhabitants of China, and also of Burma and the Philippines, grow. This, however, does not come near filling their own peacetime requirements for internal consumption. Their expansion was almost entirely dictated by the desire to be rid of the necessity of obtaining raw materials from others and by the desire to form an economic self-sufficient *bloc*.

7. Co-Prosperity or Co-Endurance?

Hence the slogan of "The Great East Asia Co-Prosperity Sphere." East Asia is to be independent or rather to be wholly dependent upon Japan. As a result of her conquests this dream has to some extent been realised. But although Japan is in possession of almost all the raw materials she now requires, shortage of shipping and the necessity of concentrating upon war production have made it impossible for her to make the raw materials now at her disposal available to the inhabitants of occupied territories, or indeed to the Japanese themselves. Hence the Japanese have been obliged to refer to the "Co-Endurance Sphere," and to tell occupied countries that they must endure much with Japan before achieving the goal of "Co-Prosperity."

V. The Myth of Invincibility

1. The Tanaka Memorial Proved Accurate

The Japanese, after the last war, intended to achieve power through economic penetration, but informed circles acquainted with the ruling circles in Japan had long seen whither her intentions would lead her. The so-called "Tanaka Memorial,"* although it was probably not by Baron Tanaka, nor was it presented to the Emperor of Japan, must nevertheless have been written by someone very intimately acquainted with Japanese policy, since subsequent events have shown its prognostications to be largely accurate. If your Emperor is a God, it would seem to follow logically that he must be prepared to rule not only his own land but the whole world, and Japanese politicians and even university professors have not been shy of expressing the most far-reaching aims. They fished out from one of their ancient chronicles the slogan *Hakko Ichiu,* which means the eight points of the compass (the traditional Japanese compass has eight points) under one roof. This slogan, far from cloaking, as the Japanese seem to consider that it does, all their ambitions, revealed them in the clearest possible light. All the world was to be subdued and to live under the Japanese roof.

2. "The Way of the Emperor" Invented

They further produced the slogan of *Kodo,* which means the way of the Emperor. This was invented to fit in with the Confucian principle of "kingly way." It therefore appears to approximate closely to the Confucian principle. Its essence is as different as possible. The king, as conceived by Confucius, was to rule through goodness; if he were good his people would be good; they would imitate him and goodness would gradually prevail throughout the land, and the neighbours, seeing this, would wish to be incorporated in so good a state. But the Japanese principle of the "way of the Emperor" is based on the Japanese assumption that their Emperor is a descendant of the Sun Goddess and that he,

---

* The 'Tanaka Memorial' was first published in a Chinese journal in 1927 and outlined Japan's strategy for world domination. Japan at the time denied that the document was genuine and its authenticity has been in dispute since.

therefore, has the right to rule over the rest of the world. Under such a programme, any piece of land which can be grabbed would contribute to the greater glory of the Emperor of Japan.

3. The Herrenvolk Complex

From all the above it will have become apparent that the main reason why the Japanese find it impossible to fit into the comity of nations lies in the idea, which they have so sedulously propagated among themselves, that they are a race apart. In this they greatly resemble the Germans, with the significant distinction that the Japanese have for so long been isolated from the rest of the world that it is much easier for them to believe wholeheartedly that they are different. Every German knows somewhere in his heart of hearts that the idea that he belongs to a Herrenvolk* is nonsense: few Japanese are aware of this. However, it is difficult for a Herrenvolk to stand up to defeat: the foundation of its people's belief in its own superiority vanishes. The Japanese are extreme realists and believe that success is the sole criterion by which their actions need be judged. If their actions succeed, they are thought to be in accordance with the will of the Emperor. If they fail, they are thought to be contrary to the will of the Emperor.

4. ... And How it can be Cured

It is therefore of paramount importance both that the Japanese military force should be decisively defeated, and that the Japanese people should be clearly aware that the military forces by their aggressive policy brought such defeat upon themselves and upon the Japanese people. It will not be very easy to bring this to the attention of the Japanese people. We had the experience after the last war of a Germany which never admitted that it had been defeated because its armed forces were able to spread with success the myth that the German home front let them down. There is

---

* *Herrenvolk*—i.e., (essentially) 'master race'.

no doubt that the Japanese military would take a similar line. For many years no Japanese, except for a few privileged officials, have been allowed to possess a short-wave wireless set. The Japanese people, therefore, have been obliged to listen only to the news as presented by their own authorities. Therefore the strictest possible censorship has prevented all news and indeed "dangerous thoughts" from percolating in from the outside world. It will, therefore, be on the whole easier for the Japanese armed forces to persuade their own people that they have not really been defeated if that suits their book.

5. And after Defeat?

It must therefore be a primary objective of the United Nations to enlighten the Japanese people on this point. There is very little doubt but that, if they really became aware that their armed aggression has failed, they will turn against their military as they turned after the last war against their "liberal democrats," who were also sensed to have failed. Once, therefore, the defeat of Japan is really accomplished, the Japanese must be shown that their armed aggression has failed but that their peacetime achievements succeeded: wherever the name of Japan is respected it is due to the artistic and industrial successes of the Japanese people; wherever the name of Japan is hated, it is due to the actions of Japanese militarists. Much nonsense is talked about the Oriental desire to "save face," but when dealing with Japanese it is essential always to provide them with a way out. It is suggested that the above might be an innocuous and a true method of doing this.

As will have been seen, very little hope could be placed upon "liberal" or "democratic" elements within Japan, but a great deal of hope may be placed upon *sensible* Japanese in all walks of life. Japan would not have risen so rapidly to such heights without using men of great shrewdness and perspicacity. We must place our hopes on them; if they realise the depths to which their militarists have brought them, they will surely attempt to find a rational way out.

WAR

Look Homeward, Jap

ABCA 'War' Pamphlet No. 85, January 6th, 1945

Don't Worry, It's Only a Snake

By Major FRANK OWEN

Reproduced by permission of the B.B.C. from a broadcast given on the Home Service on December 10th, 1944.

YOU are sitting in a forest, in the far north of Scotland, except that it is not a forest, which is a rather pleasant place—but a jungle which is not at all a pleasant place. The nearest city to you is London, which is 500 miles away. At Berwick-on-Tweed there is a large village, and somewhere about York there is a small market town, otherwise the whole of the way back to that nearest city is jungle.

If you're lucky, your home up there is a basha, which is a bamboo hut with an earthen floor. It keeps out most of the rain, some of the heat, and none of the insects. If you're unlucky, you're squatting in a foxhole under Japanese mortar fire, waiting to assault a Japanese machine-gun nest, and it's probably still raining.

Starts as a Single-track Railway

This is the Burma front. A quarter of a million British soldiers live there, fight, march, patrol there. Some have been on duty there for three years. There's a way back from the front, but it doesn't run direct between your outpost and that first big city at the base. This line of communication starts off in Kent as a single-track railway, and goes meandering over to the Hook of Holland and on up to Copenhagen, where it stops.

From there, the roadway begins. It was built by Army Engineers, shearing its path through a wilderness, clinging to the face of a precipice, winding its way up into the clouds 8,000 ft. high, and above the clouds. All the way up through Norway and across the North Sea, if the North Sea were dry land, until it reaches you in your outpost in Scotland. Or it would, if you were on the Burma front.

Along this road every day will flow, must flow, the food for the great army up forward. Do you realise that it is the largest single army in the world? For besides the British up there are Indian soldiers, Ghurkas, Americans, West Africans and East Africans, Chinese, Burmese, and the warrior hill tribes of the jungle, the Nagas, the Chins, Kachins, Karens—altogether 600,000 troops are fighting in the 14th Army, and all must eat. So every 24 hours 2,000 tons of food will go up that single-track mountain railway, and along those military roads. Motor trucks, jeeps, ox wagons, mules, donkeys, and elephants, will carry it up to the front. Though landslides block the railway or the highway and floods have swept away the bridges, supplies will get there.

War in the Jungle is an Art

War in the jungle is really first and foremost the art of keeping that road open. And secondly, it is the art of cutting the road behind the enemy, then he will die. The Japanese forgot that first law. But the men of the 14th Army learned it so well that in this year's battles along the Burma front they have killed 70,000 Japanese.

The 14th Army and the airmen of the Eastern Air Command have beaten the Japanese at something else—how to improvise a new line of supply when the existing one is broken. For on a front such as ours, 20,000 square miles of the wildest country in the whole world, it must always be possible for a party of daring raiders to penetrate your zone and cut your roads. But to-day when the Jap does this, our troops simply stand fast where they are and our aircraft feed them from the sky, dropping them their rations every day by parachute, with ammunition, weapons, medical supplies, cigarettes and even newspapers.

Three Times as High as Snowdon

In the siege of Imphal we had an entire Army Corps encircled and every road cut. The Air Forces, British and U.S., poured in supplies through the roof of the jungle, 76,000 tons of them. They brought into that battle, by air, two and a half divisions of reinforcements, with all their guns, wagons, jeeps and mules. They brought in bulldozers and even steam-rollers to make new landing-strips for the'planes. And, they took out safely 30,000 wounded.

They flew blind, through the black, monsoon mist, over those terrible mountains, three times as high as Snowdon, without a single casualty. The soldiers will never forget the Air Forces for that. At a single stroke they cut in half the suffering of the jungle war.

It is morning and you are 2,000 feet up on a gunsite in Arakan. The gunners are stripped to the belt, bronzed almost as black as their Indian and African comrades. And the horse-flies are eating their lunch off them. At sunset will come the mosquitoes, eating their supper, and bringing malaria, too, if you don't look out. When night steals up out of the plain, it will be as cold as December over here.

It is blazing noon and you belong to the infantry, the County Regiments, the Dorsets, Devons, Durhams, the Lincolns, Yorks and Lancs, the Scots and Welsh border regiments. You're slogging your way along a jungle river-bed or slashing a path foot by foot through a bamboo forest so thick that it resembles a hedge of thorns an acre deep. You've got your pack on your back and your rifle slung on the shoulder, and five days' rations, and a few hand-grenades to cart along with you, and the slope ahead is a gradient of one in two— and it's your turn to carry the bren.

Like the Jungle, a Bogy

It is night and you're on patrol. For a week you've been moving through an uncharted forest, of trees 100 ft. high with long, trailing vines, in a green darkness where curious beasts and birds and insects live. The moon makes shadows on the walls of the trees. There is an eerie sharp crackle with the bamboo branches high above you in the windless night. What was that? Or the leaves falling softly, like a footfall.

You hear birds calling to one another. They might be Japs, signalling to one another. There's a sudden, mocking laugh. It is to provoke you to laugh. Be dead silent and don't move or a stream of bullets will whip through the trees. But if you are silent the Jap will try again and he will betray his position.

Well, we, the men, know those tricks, and some better ones! The Jap, like the jungle, is a bogy. When you know him you have beaten him. He goes on repeating the pattern of all his old devices, long after we have found the answer and applied it. And the jungle. It's a place of treachery, and for those who don't know it, of terror. When you do know it, there's nothing to it.

The 14th Army soldiers have proved it a thousand times.

Burma, 1944

By Capt. F. E. FIRMINGER, A.E.C

WAR Staff Writer

IF the European events of the year 1944 may later be seen as the culmination and end of long-planned war, the events in Burma are likely to write the first chapters in the history of campaigns no less decisive, and militarily no less epoch-marking. The Burma struggle was not only different altogether from the war in the West, it was different entirely from war as it had hitherto been fought.

The fundamental principles of war cannot change, but their application to unprecedented difficulties gives them new aspects. The ground was different, the kind of enemy was different, and the call on the courage and endurance of humanity was different from anything thought possible in the twentieth century. On the one side was the Japanese enemy, long and arduously trained to carry the fight to conditions in which it was thought unlikely that modern Western men could give battle; there was no lack of heroism and resolution here.

Their army as a whole looked strange to the modern soldier; lightly clad, relying on what they could find on their way, or capture from the enemy, fired with an ancient anachronistic spirit, they were a direct throwback to old wars which seemed to have given place to other forms.

Not at Home Without Machines

Against them were men trained to rely on the appurtenances

of modern industrial civilisation, not at home without machines and appliances, brought up for the most part in mills and factories and the towns which surround them, not thought capable of the physical endurance the terrain would demand, certainly not happy away from all that modern society had trained them to regard as everyday and indispensable. And yet it was these men who imposed their will on the others, who forced them to reckon with technical industry in those savage mountains, never letting the enemy get the game into his own hands.

In the end it was our sort of war that the enemy was forced to fight—a war of supply and organisation, a war in which science exploited the resources of all the elements; and, in this sort of combat, he broke down. In itself, this alone would have guaranteed victory, and will write the story in the pages of the manuals which soldiers must learn.

The other half of the picture is that the enemy's calculation broke down in its second assumption, his belief that modern Western man was incapable of the heroism and endurance which a more generous life was supposed to have ironed out of him. Man for man the Jap soldier was outfought; not that his soldiers failed to fight up to the standard to which they had been trained.

All this and more the Japanese divisions gave; it was not enough. Against them were better men, who did enough and more to explode the credit of those who would have us believe that the effects of comfort in the daily peacetime round are the decay and disintegration of the ancient qualities which gave man his mastery over nature and the wild beasts.

The Three Campaigns of 1944

Baldly, there were three campaigns in Burma in 1944. All of them were directed by S.E. Asia Command, all of them, that is, came under what was then commanded by General Sir G. Giffard and now by General Sir Oliver Leese; two of them were fought by parts of the 14th Army, and the third was fought by a joint, and unprecedented, effort between British airborne troops under Generals Wingate and Lentaigne on the one hand and the American-trained Chinese of General Stilwell's army on the other.

The first move was ours. 15 Indian Corps (Gen. Christison) was ordered to advance into the Akyab peninsula and clear it as far south as was necessary to hold the Maungdaw-Buthidawng line and to make possible the use of the Naaf River. 15 Corps advanced down either side of the Mayu Range, until in March they were fiercely attacked by the Japanese.

Trained to Expect Encirclement

The Japanese orders clearly were to destroy 15 Corps and invade India. Their attempt was to divide Gen. Christison's forces and annihilate them. They had immediate and spectacular successes, and the flags were flown in Tokyo in March. It seemed that this British force had gone the way of others—seemed, that is, to Tokyo to have gone that way. Cool heads were kept, however, both on the spot and at G.H.Q. The men had been trained to expect encirclement, and they had now got it. Our reliance was on the power of supply by air to deny to the enemy the advantages of encirclement on the ground.

It worked; and in April and May the divisions (which contained a very high proportion of British white troops) struck back, and the Japanese were humiliatingly defeated and largely wiped out. By June, when the monsoons broke, Gen. Christison had not only achieved his objectives, but had annihilated a large Japanese force in the process. Thus the right flank of our advance into Burma was secured.

On the left, Gen. Stilwell was slowly unwinding his new Ledo Road over incredible difficulties towards the Chinese border and a junction with the old Burma Road. With it went the pipe line which was intended almost to double the carrying capacity of allied aircraft supplying Chiang Kai-shek. Gen. Wingate's airborne forces were ordered to strike behind the Japanese facing Stilwell and to hamper and immobilise them and to bring about the fall of Mogaung.

Won by the Application of Japanese Tactics

In May, Myitkyina air-strip was captured by Stilwell's Chinese, appearing from nowhere, whilst the Japanese Command sought, in confusion and without success, for Wingate's force, now commanded by Gen. Lentaigne. Myitkyina held out for two and a half months but fell in August after an epic siege. Gen. Stilwell's army, now under Gen. Sultan, pressed on to Shwegu and Bhamo, where tank country begins. If the 15 Corps' victories had been won by successful opposition to traditional Jap tactics, the campaign on the left flank had been won by the application of Japanese tactics against their sponsors, but on a scale and in a way undreamed of in Tokyo.

In the centre, the first move came from the Japanese, also in March. They crossed the Chindwin River and entered India. We were done for again (in Tokyo). The Empire was staggering, and the next shove would put it down for the count. Out came the flags.

Imphal and Kohima were surrounded and cut off. Soldiers (especially British soldiers) would never fight on when that happened. Encircled troops had to give in or die. The little Jap soldiers would be in Delhi as soon as they could stroll over the mountains. The Indians would welcome their co-Asiatic prosperity saviours. Blockheaded Gen. Mutaguchi was the chap who was doing all this.

Mainly a Business of Waving Swords

The Japanese were right enough, of course, by the standards of the old days. Encircled troops had to give in. Only these didn't. They fought it out, and got their supplies by air, from which the Jap was driven in some three days of fighting. It was not easy, of course. Major-General "Alf" Snelling was the man who did it, and it will rank for ever as the model of supply in the field in impossible conditions.

In May the garrisons were strong enough to counter-attack (after two months of annihilation by the Tokyo radio). In June Mutaguchi's main forces were caught on the Kohima-Imphal road. Those who did not die where they stood, fled in disastrous defeat down the road to Tiddim. For them, the mockers of all that the West stood for, there was no supply worked out by men who did not think of war mainly as a business of waving swords and despising all but the strong right arm.

The penalties suffered by the Jap troops were such as have seldom been exacted in the long and terrible history of war. They were run right out of India, down to Tiddim and on to Kalewa, within sight of the open tank country beyond, with all the menace that holds for the sword-waver, who at heart despises, even when he uses, the modern weapons of combat.

In these three adventures the Japs lost 70,000 men, amongst whom were more prisoners than had ever been taken before. Our own losses were less than a quarter.

The Japanese and the Future

Militarily, what had been done was about what we had set out to do. In the Arakan, on our right, we had gained the objectives we had set ourselves. In the centre we had driven the Japanese from India, and had pushed the war back to ground from which almost anything may be expected to develop. On our left, we have achieved the link-up with China which brings the third of the United Nations of the war against Japan into immediate contact on the ground with the other two. The Japanese cannot be facing his Burma future with confidence, and we might well speculate on the feelings of the enemy commanders as they turn over in their minds the fact that the Commander-in-Chief, Lord Louis Mountbatten, is primarily an Admiral, and that General Browning

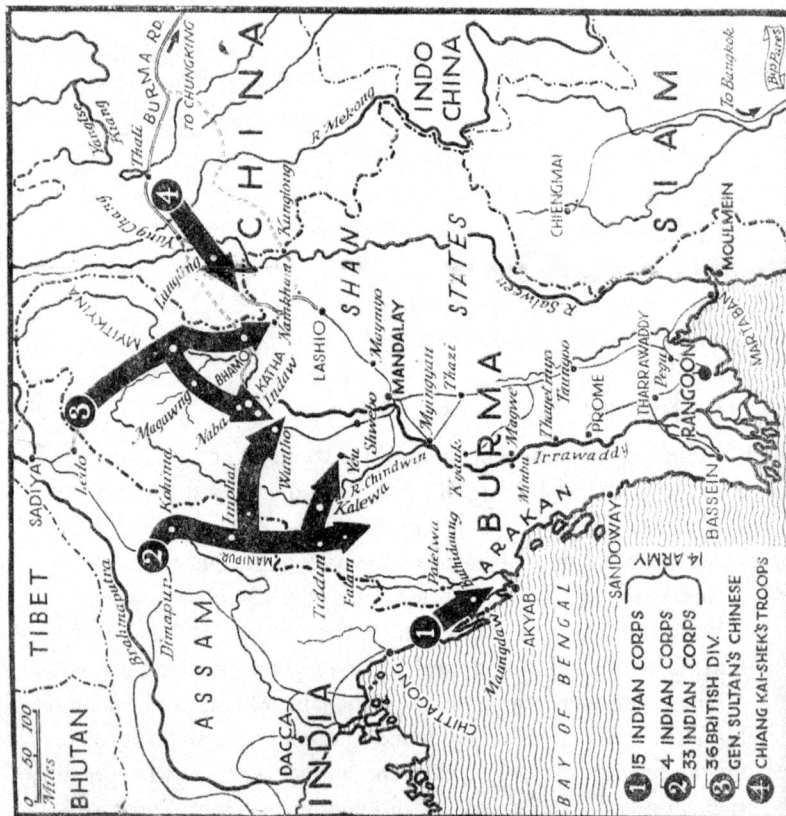

S. E. A. C.

Admiral Lord
LOUIS MOUNTBATTEN
*In command of all allied
operations*

General Sir
OLIVER LEESE
Land Operations

14th Army
Gen. SLIM

15 Indian Corps
Lt.-Gen. CHRISTISON

4 Indian Corps
Lt.-Gen. SCOONES

33 Indian Corps
Lt.-Gen. STOPFORD

Long Range Penetration Force
Maj.-Gen. LENTAIGNE

36 British Division
Maj.-Gen. FESTING

American-trained Chinese
Lt.-Gen. SULTAN, U.S.A.

① 15 INDIAN CORPS
② 4 INDIAN CORPS
③ 33 INDIAN CORPS
④ 36 BRITISH DIV
  GEN. SULTAN'S CHINESE
  CHIANG KAI-SHEK'S TROOPS

of Arnhem is on the spot as Chief of Staff. By now, too, the Jap will know that we had to start the Burma campaign of 1944 with very much less force than had been originally intended, for a large part of what Admiral Mountbatten had been expecting was at the last moment diverted to the affairs of Europe. It is unlikely that the Jap command expects quite so much indirect help from the other end of the Axis in 1945.

The Jap Soldier Knows Now

In armies things have a wonderful way of getting around; the jungle telegraph has nothing on it. Some of the things that will be going the rounds in the Japanese Army we can guess at. What is the greeting now to the chap straight from home who starts talking about the decadence of white soldiers? What do Jap sentries feel like at night when the word goes round that Nagas, Kachins or Karens are also having a look round that night? And what do Jap Generals, who not so long ago were ascribing their supremacy in war to perfectly combined land, sea and air operations, feel when someone has the bad taste to mention General Wingate? We have said that some 70,000 Japanese won't be there to feel anything, but enough of them got away from the campaigns of 1944 to let the rest have a rough idea of what to expect.

In Burma, the Way was Found

But the physical figures mean nothing when put side by side with the great historical decisions which these campaigns had made. The setting, and the questions at stake, were worthy of the unparalleled human endeavour and bravery that had been cast into the account. The Jap is not beaten yet, but in Burma the way was found, and fundamental problems were solved.

Had the answer been the one worked out in Tokyo, the war against Japan would have been lost, and, at a blow, the world would have lost with it the achievements of centuries of patient progress and unshakable affirmation of right and wrong. Let us try to see what some of those problems were.

The first has already been seen. It was fundamental to the whole Japanese reason for being in the war at all that there existed on their side profound and unalterable virtues which could not be resisted by moral or material force. For example:—

The Jap Claim

They were Asiatics, fighting for Asia, and wanted by Asia.

They were divinely appointed to destroy the British Empire.

Their way of life, their conception of poverty as a good in itself, gave them unmatched advantages over the whites.

Defeat, hitherto unknown to their armies, was a divinely decreed impossibility.

Their way of fighting war was a more skilful way than ours; their generals better generals, their strategy better strategy, their organisation better organisation.

None of these theories stood up to the test.

It will be seen that, added together, they amount to the affirmation of the claim that all that has happened to mankind in the West for centuries has been a move backward, away from strength and virtue, and that the emergence of Japan, which had retained all those ancient virtues and had mastered what was worth learning from the rest, was a signal for taking the path back without losing anything worth keeping. Let us consider them one by one.

The Japanese Fantasies

(a) *Asia for the Asiatics*

For this to have worked out well for the Japs, it would have been necessary for our Indian troops not to have fought, but either to have deserted or mutinied. It should certainly have been impossible for us to have transported powerful African forces to

Asia to take part in the fight against a common enemy.

But the Indian troops did fight, and showed a peculiar and undivine determination to whip off Japanese heads and to place bullets firmly through Japanese hearts. Moreover, vast numbers of labourers could be found to help in the work of supply. In an army of 700,000 there is, of course, a preponderance of Asiatics, and these men have been prepared to suffer unmeasurable hardship in the fight, and to be led into battle by British officers, and to enter into rivalry in daring and resolution with British troops.

Not for Asiatics from Tokyo

Moreover, the Indian army, unlike our own, consisted solely of volunteers. They all wanted to be in the war against Japan. If Asia was to be for the Asiatics, then, it was, as a bare minimum, not to be for Asiatics from Tokyo. If the British Empire was to go, it was not to be replaced by a Japanese co-prosperity sphere. Whatever the Asiatic was fighting for, it had nothing to do with the august virtues of the Sun-Goddess. The age of enlightenment and the path back were still not in sight.

No doubt the Japanese will continue to plug the co-prosperity sphere line, for they are, as a nation, not very fluid-minded, but apprehension as to its results will now be replaced by admiration of the sheer cold-blooded impudence behind it.

(b) *The Divine Mission*

Though the Japanese entry into the war was made by means of the Pearl Harbour attack on the U.S., Japanese long-distance thought has not concentrated so much on the Americans as on the British.

If they were to rule the world, they would have to contrive to be, in some way or other, our heirs and successors in a very large part of it.

They could observe, also, that whatever it was that held the British Empire together, it certainly was not force. That left either self-interest among the members of the Empire, or some special moral qualities, universally recognised, which made men want to be in it. They even had Hitler's word for a good deal of this.

They consequently claimed both, the co-prosperity sphere and the august virtues. There was also a suggestion that, if these wouldn't do, they could supply the force of arms which we had not got.

The Excitement was in Tokyo

The approach, therefore, of Japanese armies towards India, and the sacred crossing of the frontiers should surely have been some sort of signal, either of approaching well-being or of the coming of God. Contrary to expectations, it caused remarkably little stir; most of the excitement was in Tokyo. Everyone else was more interested in what was going on in Europe.

The Japanese could wait; no doubt they could be held up by the very small part of our united strength which was available for the task. Difficult? But we have had this sort of difficulty for some centuries. We have had to deal with people like Mutaguchi before; no doubt our ingenuity and persistence will not be beyond dealing with them again. As a very tiny irreduceable demand, Tokyo might have expected more space in our newspapers.

We had even had the temerity to divert a great part of the supplies intended for use against the Japs into action at Anzio, and there were no reports of the stuff sinking at the shame of this comedown.

The Divine Mission didn't show up very well in the event.

(c) *The Jap Superiority as a Soldier*

Extremely arduous training has made the Jap rank and file soldier first class. The training is not only physically long and taxing, but it makes equally heavy spiritual demands. The result of all this is to produce a most formidable fighting man, on whom the Japanese conception of war has learned to rely.

Their high command has thought always in terms of better man for man conditions being a major factor in their strategy. Their choice of ground and their timing would not normally be considered sound, but are accepted as such in view of the demands they are able to make on their men.

It is typical of the Japanese that, for him, the way to fight should be to expend the greatest amounts of the cheapest material, which in this case are human lives. Material costs more and is harder to invent and manage. The rifle gets more tender and humane consideration, is surrounded by more august rites, than the man. When he reports for duty, there are no flags out for him; but when he gets his rifle, a pompous little ceremony is held over the event.

No Luxury, Little Comfort

Most Japanese fighting troops come from the farms, where life is hard. There is no luxury, there is little comfort. Both of these commodities are represented to him as weak; his country has built up its armaments with imports bought on the strength of the profits made out of his cheap labour. Agricultural austerity is a permanent feature of Japanese government policy. Against this background, the army is not so bad. The Jap claims it to be an ideal training and virtuous, endowing his troops with special qualities, which, of course, it does: the clash of opinion can occur only when one examines the evil of the thing.

It is also axiomatic with Jap army thinkers that Western ways soften and destroy the morale, and man for man, their fellows, brought up in their way, will be better than ours. And the more difficult the ground, the more impossible it is to reinforce human effort with complicated material, the greater will be their advantage.

Burma should thus have been an unqualified success. Leaping from crag to crag, bounding from sea-level to 9,000 feet, their soldiers should have outmatched us. And leap they did, bound as never before. They cut us off, they ran all round us, but it still wasn't good enough.

Because He was Brave

The morale opposed to all this did not crack.

In the end it was the Japanese who fell back, not because the Jap private soldier had given up, but because human strength and endurance could not take what we were able to offer in reply. The lessons of Burma drove home the suggestion of New Guinea, which was that the Jap had made a fatal miscalculation in thinking that because he was brave, we must be cowards.

Overwhelmed by the Russians

The Jap claims never to have suffered defeat.

This is not quite true, as he was thrown out of Korea 350 years ago by the Chinese, and was defeated at sea by the Koreans, but still, in modern times, he has not done so badly. He was over-whelmed by the Russians at Nomonhan in a little incident just before this war which cost him an admitted 18,000 killed, and the Chinese have occasionally, as at Taierchwang, thrown him back in disorder. Apart from that he has mostly been able to claim the tactical victory of holding the ground he has once occupied.

In Burma, after great and much advertised claims, he was hurled back and driven down the mountains in disastrous rout. Having entered India, and thus made that part of the earth semi-sacred, he was most bloodily ejected. "It is very regrettable" said Gen. Mutaguchi, which didn't seem much from a Commander who had just lost a major campaign.

Speed Up Their Suicide Tendencies

Some Japs, not a vast number, even gave themselves up in despair, and this was a new thing for them. Even if it does not get into the Jap newspapers, an event of this sort is known to the troops, and is mentioned in Army orders. There is no knowing what will happen once the thing catches on; it might even become very regrettable indeed.

One cannot forecast the Japanese reaction to defeat. There are some who know them well who think that it would accentuate and speed up their suicide tendencies; there are others who think that, confronted with this new thing often enough, they would crack altogether. Others feel that it would only stir them to greater efforts. On the whole it is safer to accept this last as the most probable result.

A Third-class Army of First-class Men

Discussion of all the factors we have so far looked at can only be largely speculative and academic. When, however, we look at the concrete comparison of their army with ours, we have something to get our teeth into, something that it is now impossible for the Jap to do very much to remedy.

The Jap army in Burma was described as a third-class army of first-class soldiers, and this is very much the chief lesson of the campaigns. Behind their army lay all that they thought it proper to put into the effort of modern war, or all that they could contrive to put in. Fighting men are one part of the picture, but they can do only so much; their heroism must be conditioned by the weapons they are given to be heroic with, by the rations that keep up their strength, and by the brains that co-ordinate their moves with those of their fellowmen. We have said enough about the men; it is time to look at the material and the leadership.

They Underestimated Us

The purpose of surrounding an enemy is to cut him off from his supplies. In the past this has been done by physical encompassment on the ground, and the Japs had got that far in their military manuals. What they overlooked, or discounted, was what could be done by air, so that, whilst at Arakan and at Kohima and Imphal, they pulled off the encirclement, and held on long enough to have starved out ordinary armies with no other link, they had apparently made wildly insufficient preparation for an air campaign and they were driven from the air in very little time.

Our supplies came in. Or, again, it may have been that, estimating what was and was not possible by their own standards, they had thought that the amount of organisation needed to bring in what we did was beyond human ingenuity. If that is so, their ideas of relative ingenuity must have undergone some fundamental changes, and have caused considerable misgiving as to their own share of it. There is nothing more fatal to commanders than the feeling that the man opposed to them is too clever for them.

Their Way and Ours

This was meeting the Japanese way of fighting with our own; it was opposing meticulous organisation and hairbreadth calculation to wild and savage dash. It was adapting and bringing up to date the methods which had won former wars for us, but had looked like losing this one. It was, if you like, relying on an old friend. We do it that way because it is our way, to which we automatically look in times of urgent stress.

But the Japanese had given us another clue to their view of war. In the early days they had shown that infiltration and surprise were their major weapons, and the betting was that they thought so highly of these ways because they themselves feared them most. It throws the other side off the drill book, back, frequently enough, on to each man's own individual resources, his own particular ingenuity and courage.

If the Jap thought so much of this, it was at least worth trying out against him, in a way and on a scale that he had not tried. Thus Major-General Wingate's long-range penetration force was raised to experiment with this sort of warfare and Jap reactions to it. They would encircle and cut off, they too would move so quickly that the Jap would never know where they might next turn up, but instead of doing it on foot or by sea, they would use the air.

So Unsuitable to Expectant Conquerors

The reactions of the Japanese commanders to all this proved the point; they were exactly what our own reactions had been expected by the Japs to be. This kind of warfare, therefore, was taking the Japanese lesson and turning it against them. Once again, its effect must have been to give the Jap just that inferiority complex about us that is so unsuitable to expectant world-conquerors, and to remind him of all the stories he has ever heard about people who lose the first few years of war and win the last.

The net result of all the factors we have taken into consideration here cannot be estimated as anything else but overwhelming. Let each man think back to his feelings at the flood tide of Japanese success, early in 1942, and ask himself how his feelings to-day compare, and how it is that he arrived at so profoundly changed a view.

The Australian successes in New Guinea were the giant's fingers that started the ball rolling, and the American successes at sea were the beacons which first lighted up hopes of peace such as we would accept in measurably close order. But the British campaigns of Burma, 1944, may well be the record to which each one who shares the glory of the achievement will point as the real crux and turning point of the war against Japan.

CURRENT AFFAIRS

Japanese Purpose

ABCA 'Current Affairs' Pamphlet No. 86, January 13th, 1945

JAPANESE PURPOSE

By Capt. F. E. Firminger, A.E.C.

THE first question that most people want to have answered about Japan and the Japanese War is "How long will it last?" We can't answer that one. There are a few others that we can attempt, however, such as: What sort of man is the Jap? What is he like at home? What got such a little man into such a big war? What does he expect to get out of it? What would things be like if we let him get away with it? Let us take them in order.

What Sort of Man is the Jap?

Wild Beasts from the Mountains

When Gen. Homma, the man who led the Japanese attack on the Philippines, was asked by journalists why his men behaved so badly at Tientsin, where he was C.-in-C. at the time they were stripping white women at the barriers, he made the off the record answer, "The mistake you make is to think of them as human beings. They are not. They are wild beasts from the mountains." Now, the General had spent a good many years in the West, and he may have been impressed by certain differences in conduct there and in his own country. He may have met, for example, the Colonel in his own army, who was chief military instructor at a Japanese High School, and who was surprised and bitterly disillusioned to hear that the process of having babies which he had hitherto regarded as exclusively Japanese was common to all mankind. Like so many regular soldiers in Japan, he knew nothing at all except the raw business of fighting. He, no doubt, was one of the "On, on, to Delhi" boys who forgot all about the rations in their latest attacks on India.

Those 10,000,000 Casualties

We need not go so far, however, as Gen. Homma in condemning the Japanese soldier. He has human strengths and weaknesses not shared by the wild beasts; strengths that come from arduous and intelligent training, weaknesses that arise from living, after all, in a human society, and must be conquered if the approved standard of barbarity is to be achieved. It is one of the favourite tricks of Jap leaders to try to frighten the world by painting the picture of their own indifference to death and discomfort. One of their Admirals, in a cosy little chat with an American officer before the war, suddenly said, "We are prepared to lose ten million men. How many are you prepared to lose?" That was meant to scare the Westerner, and the Jap may have started this war in the hope that considerations of that sort would lead us to a negotiated peace after enough blood had been let. But if the Jap estimate of ten million casualties to themselves is their limit, it doesn't look like being enough the way things are going these days, because the event is beginning to show that the Japanese have to lose a good many men before accounting for one of ours. In any case the Jap Admiral would not have put things quite that way to his own people, who also have wives, children, homes that they would like to see again. None the less, the Jap is prepared to suffer immense losses, and nothing shows better than this the evil of a government which throws into the scale of political gain this immense disregard for human life and suffering—not only of the lives and suffering of others but of its own people, who put their trust in their leaders.

A Letter from Home

The Jap soldier, for half a century now, has been trained to believe that the function of a soldier is to get himself killed in battle as the shortest cut to heaven. There is a famous letter, familiar to every Jap school-child, taken off the body of a dead Jap soldier in the Manchurian war of 1905-6, from his mother, upbraiding him with the fact that he had so far failed to honour the Emperor and himself by getting himself killed. This is held out as a national example of right thinking, but the soldier, being a human being, is bound to ask himself from time to time how far he approves of the sort of view from the old folks at home. The Jap High Command has been a bit bothered by it themselves, it appears, since it began to dawn on them that this was co-operation with our own war aims at a very vital level, and they have had the job of trying to talk themselves and their men into a different frame of mind, one that would be at the same time sufficiently august, but a shade more economical of man-power and material. Of one thing we may be certain, both by logical reasoning and from the evidence at our disposal. The soldier who has been subjected to this sort of propaganda will not be a frightfully gay chap in the intervals between fighting and atrocity.

Taking On the Champion

In fact the Jap soldier is more subject to homesickness than most. He was narrowly brought up, and taught to value the in-

expensive pleasures of viewing his
own little countryside, and when
he is deprived of that, he is without
resources to keep himself amused.
He is usually, like our own soldiers,
fighting in a country entirely different from his own, but without
the long Imperial tradition which
we have, which teaches a man that
high standards of life and morality
sometimes demand long journeys
and great sacrifice in defence of them. The Jap has little knowledge of the world outside Japan, and is taught to hate it. More
than us, he is frightened by what is strange, and he has the ev-
erlasting disadvantage of the challenger. Like the man who has
won a few good local fights, and is now assured by his manager
that the time has come to get into the ring against the hitherto
undefeated champion, he sometimes wonders. His manager tells
him that everything will be all right, but he can't help letting his
mind wander over our unbeaten record, for he is the man who
has to take it on the chin.

Nobody Loves Them

He doesn't get along well in other people's countries. Most
Europeans who have been to Japan, on the other hand, have enjoyed themselves, for they were nearly always fairly well off, and
consequently found themselves near the top of the semi-feudal
system there, and that, as long as one's conscience does not get one
around to thinking about the chap at the bottom, is an extremely
comfortable place to be. The Jap behaves better at home; it is when
he goes abroad that the trouble starts. If he goes as an army he
is able to express his dislike for any other system than his own,
and to begin to meddle with it. It is this which has so bitterly
disillusioned the quislings who accepted the Jap as a liberator.

These people did not like the British Empire in the days when they had no experience of the alternatives, but they have come to value the cardinal principle of British imperialism, which is to leave the people undisturbed in their own ways as long as these ways are peaceful.

The Chinese always has charm, even when he cannot read or write, and works all day at a job no Westerner would stomach. No race is more universally recognised as free from charm than the Japanese. They have themselves recognised this failing, and appreciated its seriousness, so far as to have invited at considerable expense the author of a best-selling work on how to win friends and influence people,* to come over and show them how to do it. He abandoned the task pretty soon after the Japanese had started to get to work influencing people in China. But the Jap still wishes to please, and is rather like the German who shed tears in Shanghai on being cut dead by a Dutchman the day after Rotterdam. He just couldn't understand that what his countrymen had done went for him, too, and was unforgivable; he just knew that nobody loved him. Nobody loves the Jap, and he doesn't like it either.

Sticking to the Book

Formidable soldier though he is then, resolute and well trained, he has his weaker side as an individual. Militarily his weakness is that he is lost without the book. The fact that his own favourite enterprise was infiltration gives us the clue here. Because he does not like to have to deal with the unforeseen himself, and is lost when confronted with it, so he supposes that his enemy will be thrown into irreparable confusion once he pushed off the exact page and line of the Field Service Pocket Book, but perhaps he has

* Dale Carnegie, author of *How to Win Friends and Influence People*, made a series of visits to Japan. In July 1939 his sojourn was at the request of the Japanese Board of Tourist Industry and Japanese Government Railways which sought his counsel on how to improve communications and understanding between Japan and the USA.

begun to think that one out again since General Wingate showed him a thing or two on those lines. The British soldier is never more at home than when things go wrong; the good old Army tradition of having to think up something else because the admin. has been a shade under 100 per cent. is the most realistic form of training. It is the enemy's business to interfere with admin., and he will sometimes succeed, with the result that the soldier has to work things out for himself. He feels that normality has at last supervened. The Jap is bewildered and anxious, and will almost certainly shed a few tears. But he will still fire resolutely back at anyone who stands up and offers him a handkerchief to dry them.

Does the Jap soldier believe himself to be some sort of god? It is hard to say; national propaganda, of course, requires him to believe that he is, and failure to do so would be roughly equivalent to failing to carry out Part I orders, but it does involve a certain strain on his credulity, especially when he has to accept that the first Jap Emperor was the great-great-grand-nephew of the Sun-Goddess, which in tropical countries may not strike him as a particularly good thing to have been. Their present Emperor has occasionally been brave enough to give some slight public indication of his dislike of being constantly shadowed by bevies of lieutenant-generals, and this cannot altogether have escaped the eye of all. What the Jap really believes, nobody can say; about what he can say, however, we can be certain. He can say nothing unless he swallows the thing whole.

The Jap at Home

They are mostly farmers. Most of the fighting troops are farmers. They are far more Oriental than Western, whereas the man from the great towns, who is mostly either back at home in munitions or in the service corps, is more Western than Oriental in many respects. Life is hard for the Eastern agriculturist. Once he has left school at 14, and before he has left, back-breaking work in the field claims him for life. He has probably watched his sisters being sold off to the brothels or the great textile factories once they had reached 14 or 15 years of age, to help pay the crushing load of interest on the fantastic debts which hang round the necks of nearly all Oriental farmers. Unlike the townsman, he probably enjoyed his spell of military service, tough though that was. It was a relief from being bent double all day up to his knees in a mixture of water and manure for ever planting rice, and getting nothing for it. He doesn't get anything which would be recognised by any other country as pay when he gets into the Army—but the means are regular, the hours no worse, and he is offered a somewhat higher ideal, as he sees things, than turning out rice for next to nothing.

The Army is a Political Party

The Army is also a political party. Most of the officers are farmers, like the men, and many of them have risen from the ranks. Not all of them are like Gen. Araki, who started as the brewer's errand boy and wound up as Baron Araki with his son at, of all places, Oxford. Gen. Koiso, the present Prime Minister, for example, has a full programme of social and industrial reform which would, he hopes, have the effect of turning Japan into a country of small village communities still unable to maintain in that way a heavy industry capable of making war, but enabling the farmer to keep his daughters at home. He believes, too, that all land should be returned to the Emperor, who theoretically once owned it all, and still owns a very large part of it. The effect of that would be, of course, that the Army would own it, for during many centuries the Emperor of Japan was either an obscure and remote priest selling his autograph for a living to anyone who was interested or else a puppet in the hands of military dictators. He is back in that ancient role again now.

The Farmer and the Industrial System

The Japanese farmer hates the industrial system, and the West, which, he supposes, forced it on Japan. There is perhaps no more pathetic economic policy in the world today than that which, in Japan, seeks on the one hand to put back the clock a century to the old village life, and to maintain a war industry on the other. The plight of the farmer in all this is bad; he knows that it is he who works hard to keep the price of rice down so that the towns-man can be paid wages so low that the rest of the world cannot compete with his export product. But if he goes to China, and most Japanese soldiers will have been there, he will see farmers working at an even lower level, in conditions in which he himself would hardly keep a horse, and he will begin to think that things are not so bad after all, and a glow of pride will fill him as, if he is a good soldier, he ascribes all of this to his Emperor's manifest virtues, and when his officers tell him that Japan's mission is to do the Chinese a bit of good, as many of them do, he can at least observe that there is plenty of scope for this form of effort. When he is further informed that the plight of the Chinese is entirely due to Western materialistic money-grabbing, this strikes just the right note with him.

Japanese Private—Infantry. *German type pack with rain-coat rolled and strapped over blanket roll. Mess tin, cartridge pouch, haversack, water-bottle and entrenching tool and handle. Respirator, A.-G., is slung under the left arm.*

The Master Race

It is this which encourages the Japanese in their master-race theories. To the casual observer of Japan, it would seem hard to believe that there is much in Japanese conditions to warrant their faith, but what one must bear in mind is the Oriental background, in which the achievement of Japan seems monumental. After all, too, the only manufactured goods which fall into Japanese hands are made, in Japan, and when locks fail to work or spades come apart in his hand, how is the Jap worker to know that all locks and all spades are not subject to these tedious shortcomings? How is he to know, even, that what seems to him luxury would not be tolerated in the West as unendurable hardship? Like the Colonel and his child-production theories, he knows no other and thinks all to be exclusively Japanese and the best.

A Man's World

The Oriental world, and above all the Jap world, is a world for men. Daughters are a misfortune. Their first function is to honour their brothers, and if in this process they get sold off to the brothel in order to pay for his schooling, she has the honour of setting in the balance against the wreckage of her own life the making of his. If she avoids this duty, and gets married, her new job is now to honour her husband and his children, his male children; she can do what she likes with the girls. She will walk, respectfully, one pace behind him if they go out together, and will get up and open doors and light cigarettes for him and his men friends as required. She will stand in buses and trams while he sits down.

Yet it would be a mistake to imagine that in Japanese women there will be a considerable reservoir of hatred of the system which keeps them to this way of life. No doubt, for a few years after the last war when there was a moment when Japan seemed to be developing democratically, many a poor girl had her heart broken by the comparison between life on the American movies and life with the man she had to marry. At that time, on a ship which had at last got within sight of the coast of Japan, all the men present wept very respectably with emotion at the sight. One woman wept too; coming back after ten years in Europe, she knew what was now in store for her. But the farmer's wife, and the worker's wife have no such weaknesses. They know their job. They have probably done a spell in the brothels or the mills before marriage, and found the life there easier than in the fields, and it is they who will indicate their daughters' duty when the time comes. It is the women, too, who bring up the men, who buy them toy swords and toy machine guns, the two favourites with the Jap toy-makers. It is they who, within the limits of their poverty, give what preference there is to the boy.

Bringing Up the Soldier

Japanese male heads are never smacked, nor bottoms kicked. The first impression of most Englishmen who go to Japan is of the urgent need for this, and the dire results of its absence. In the little boys whom one sees in the streets one can discern the causes of war. Whether they believe themselves divine or not, whether they are old enough to consider the evidence or not, their standard of conduct, their pushing lack of consideration, their immediate resort to tears when thwarted, tell a grim story of what to expect of them when they grow up. It is nothing out of the way to see a little boy of three or four or even more, in a tram get hold of his mother's breast and start sucking, in spite of her feeble reproaches. Is he after all not a potential soldier?

Suicide

Suicide is a great national sport. It is not quantity, unfortunately, in peacetime for which the Japanese go, for their suicide rates are lower than several other countries. It is quality, and quality here consists of causing the maximum inconvenience to one and all of your friends. If you are a samurai, the privilege of harakiri is yours, and the snag about this is, that you only make a sort of ceremonial scratch on your stomach, while your best friend has the messy job of whipping off your head with your big sword, or of shooting you with your revolver if you are in the army. Now, this is a most inconsiderate thing to ask a friend to do, and it is also a nuisance if, being unqualified for the honour of harakiri, you adopt the popular method of jumping into a volcano. It isn't quite what it sounds. Instead of the first stop being the flames of hell below, it is all too often a ledge some twenty feet down, on which one arrives with a twisted ankle, a changed mind and a loud cry for help. If those who arrive to watch the fun fail in their exhortations to you to be a man and see the job through, and have to pull you up, you will have failed to have gained as much face as you might otherwise have acquired, but you will have succeeded in your primary objective of calling attention to yourself.

They Work in Groups

The calm, inscrutable Oriental, of whom so much has been heard, is hardly to be found in Japan. Most national ideals turn out to be hopes rather than realities, and so it is that inscrutability is so much admired by the Japanese largely because they have not got it. Their way of thought is direct and simple, it is measured in terms of what they want, and though they have cunning, it is already being shown to be of a rather elementary sort, and certainly not more than we, in our way, can outmatch and forestall. In the whole history of Japan, there are very few moments associated with the names of one or two great men, but there are countless instances of effective and powerful group action. They prefer to work in groups, they dodge individual responsibility, and cases have been known in Jap military history of serious delay caused on the death of a person in command by the hesitation of the next senior in assuming authority. This frame of mind has had its strengths as well as its weaknesses, for at times of national disaster, such as in the frequent floods, fires, earthquakes and typhoons, a splendid united effort has quickly restored the situation. At the moment of crisis, however, they are weak, and require time to get their second wind; and nothing is more fundamental in war against them than to give them no chance to take stock, but to pile new situations on top of each other.

How Did the Japs Get Into the War?

The Jap claim is that, having been forced against their will to open up their ports to the world in the middle of the last century, they then foresaw and put the responsibility on the West, that

they would industrialise themselves, with all that that meant. As they saw it, industrialisation meant an expanding population, a need for raw materials and markets, none of which existed in Japan, and the acquisition of colonial territories. Quite deliberately they set out to get these things. They needed an army, a navy, an industrial system, and a national spirit, for feudal states know nothing of patriotism; there is only the loyalty of a man to his lord, and of the lord to the overlord. In all these matters they copied the best existing models, as they saw them. Their national religion was either Buddhist, which is wildly unsuitable, with its rejection of salvation, and hope of annihilation, to an expanding and resurgent community, or Shinto, which in those days was the worship of the local divinities of the woods and the streams, frequently interspersed, and even confused, with ancestor worship. Something altogether more respectable than that would have to be contrived, and they toyed with the idea of Christianity. In the end they really invented Emperor worship to take the place of all this. The Emperor had formerly been a figure of some ceremonial importance but quite hidden from all but a few courtiers, and unknown to the people as a whole.

The Rising Standard of Living

The result of it all was much as the Japanese had expected. Industrialisation meant a rising standard of life, and the population doubled itself. The new system of government worked well because it was automatic, and there was nobody in Japan with any political tradition to contest it. The people learnt to read and write, a conscious military effort on the part of the government, who had absorbed the great lessons of the West, which all taught that the educated soldier would beat the uneducated. They saw too that in their autocratic system, the government could put over anything it wanted the people to believe, and so national education sank into national propaganda. To every problem, the government supplied the right answer. The others were all wrong, and punishable. By this means patriotism was put over, in spite of civil war. The first Emperor had been a relation of divinity, so all his descendants were, and eventually, every single Japanese was pretty divine, because he was part of the Imperial family. All virtue springs from the Emperor, and all right. If you are presented to the Emperor, you will be advised in terms not simply advisory, that if you do not keep your head bent as he enters you will be blinded by the light of his manifest virtues.

The Emperor Over All

All Oriental Emperors claim to rule everything under the

sun, either in fact or ideally. The Japanese claim, in view of the Emperor's ancestry, is particularly strong, and whether the Japs swallow the whole story or not, on this point they are resolute; their function is to rule the world, and they have failed in their duty to the Emperor if they have failed to advance his rule towards that end. The hollowness and sheer dishonesty of Jap talk of Asia for the Asiatics, the East Asia Co-Prosperity Sphere, India for the Indians, in face of their own urgently pursued religious belief that all things are for the Emperor of Japan, and their ability to persuade some quislings to accept their promises, must be such as to cause Goebbels to feel that, after all, a further fortnight at night-school taking the Jap course on this would not be a bad thing. But, in their own frequently expressed propaganda, the Japs have here a sure passport to war for just as long as they hold it or as we reject the claim they make on behalf of their Emperor.

Population Problem

More sensibly, as many people have thought, the Japs have claimed to be overpopulated, and to need more room to live. This would have looked better if the Jap had ever shown any tendency towards mass emigration unless thrust into it by his army; it would have looked better still if they had not impressed on Japanese mothers the need for having more and ever more children, and making birth control illegal. But it would have looked best of all if, instead of spending almost the whole of the results of their export trade on importing armaments, they had spent it on food for their people. Just so long, therefore, as the Japanese claim that they must eat and use only what is grown in Japan, but that other people must use what Japan sends them, war is certain.

Poverty as a Virtue

Poverty is held up in Japan by the army as a virtue. The comfortable man cannot be a good man; virtue lies only in having no means beyond bare subsistance. No Jap military government has ever for one instant tolerated talk of prosperity, except for a brief moment of Tojo, under German inspiration, on the strength of the loot which the bandit chieftain fatally allowed his countrymen to sit down and enjoy. Poverty is an impossible doctrine in the modern world wherein nearly the whole of civilised humanity is agreed on one thing alone—that the object of government is to secure the maximum comfort, security and prosperity for its people. It is hard to believe that a great power could hold any other view, but in Japan we have an example, and as long as they hold it or tolerate the holding of it by that section of its community which also has the guns, war with the West was inevitable, and it was better to have it now than later, for the Japanese have enough talent, with their numbers, to force down the standard of living of the whole world, as they forced down Lancashire, if allowed to go their own way.

Great Britain Is the Enemy

If these were the long-term causes of war, or some of them, the immediate cause is easy enough to see. In the way of all people who believe, as the Japanese believe, in poverty, in standardisation of thought, in intolerance of others, there is one major bar. The world as a whole is an Anglo-Saxon world, inasmuch as the majority of its inhabitants are either living in an Anglo-Saxon government or under the profound influence of Anglo-Saxon ideas. The whole message which we have offered the world is the contrary of all Japanese beliefs. No one people is divinely appointed to rule. If we have ruled large parts of the world, it has never been so much by force of arms as by the sheer inability of people to find anything they have liked better, and the certainty that when they do, as far as we are concerned, they can have it. The purpose of government is to achieve prosperity; poverty is an evil; and we applaud a change which turns out a government which fails to measure up to our requirements. In Japan it would be sacrilege. We have succeeded in so separating our military and political forces that the former is the servant of the latter, and the latter the servant of the people. The Jap has managed the exact opposite; the army rules the government, and the government rules the people who had no share in its making, for the elected politician has no power. If Japan's plan were to succeed the British Empire must go; they knew, too, that America regarded the existence of the British Empire as fundamental to the existence of their own way of life. To attack the one, for the Japs, with their well-understood ideas, was to attack the other.

The Two Ideas

Inasmuch as there was division of opinion in Japan about the need for attacking the Anglo-Saxon world, it was a difference only of method. Whereas the army thought, as it was their professional interest to think, that the thing could best be done by war, there were others who thought in terms of economic expansion, a phrase once popular with the navy. They saw a tremendous drive economically on the Asiatic continent and in the islands to the south, and their view was that in those parts were inexhaustible stores of raw materials and of labour that could be got together and organised by the Japs in such a way as to put the rest of the world out of business. For they saw that if people with few demands had efficiency comparable with that of people demanding more, the former must put the latter out of business, and, in any case, force them down to the lower standard. There were two motives, therefore: on the one hand, the extreme Japanese jealousy of our better position, and on the other, the prospect of loot and power in the process of organising labour amongst, say, the Chinese, where £1 a month is a good wage, and where conditions which we would regard as intolerable are not unacceptable, and where men will live as we would not keep a horse.

The Effect of Jap Competition

In terms of everyday life we can see the process. The radio, the cinema, the summer holiday—these would be the first to go as undesirable indulgence. The working day would grow longer, as men fought to keep pace with unending Oriental toil, and children would start doing half-skilled work in the home, in the evening, to keep up the family budget. This has been the process in Japan for some years, in spite of her increasing trade. There is a place for Japan, surely enough, selling her cheap goods to people who have things the Jap wants, and unable to buy better stuff, as long as the effect of this is to raise the standards of both parties, and, consequently, of the world. But there is no place for any country who ploughs back its profit, not on the rich soil of its own people, but into armament with which to make war on the rest of the world.

Tojo's Moment

Every Japanese who thought in terms of an expanding Japan, thought in terms of an eventual war with the British Empire. The only problem was—when? No doubt the majority of Japs did not, on Dec. 7, 1941, share Gen. Tojo's view that the moment had come, and that was why the whole thing had to be carried out as a secret blow, secret perhaps even from some members of the Jap Cabinet, but the whole nation applauded as one man when, for a moment, Tojo seemed to have pulled it off, and the whole of our Eastern Empire lay at his feet. That they have now set their feet on the path of irretrievable defeat, hardly anyone doubts, and that they never had the force successfully to challenge us over a long war is clear, and they must have known it at the time. What then was their hope?

They may have seen the situation in one of three ways. If they foresaw a German victory, and at that time the Germans were claiming that the Russians had thrown in their last reserves—it will be remembered that this was followed almost immediately by large scale German retreats from Moscow and Rostov—the Japanese may have felt that this was the time for a grand pincer movement right around the British Empire, which would yield them the whole of our eastern possessions as their booty. The idea of German outright victory, however, was not popular in Tokyo for they saw that complete German victory would be followed by an attack on Japan. There cannot be two master races.

It was unlikely that they foresaw a British victory, but for anybody who did, then December, 1941, was the last moment to strike at the British Empire. Mr. Churchill had left no doubt as to our intentions towards Japan, when at the moment of our greatest weakness they had forced us to close the Burma Road. Finally, and perhaps most universally in Japan, drawn battle was foreseen. For those who thought this way, December, 1941, may have appeared to be the "golden opportunity" for securing as much of the British Empire as possible whilst our hands were still full in Europe. They would have reasoned, after a drawn battle with Germany, a battle which would only have ended by reason of the exhaustion on both sides, that we should have been in no condition to go out after Japan and get back what they had taken from us. Furthermore, officially, in Tokyo, we were old and worn out, not really interested in our Empire, not prepared to make sacrifices for Australia, Burma or Malaya. All these places the Japanese thought we had come to regard as too far off and too much bother to claim the interest of a decadent race.

Jap Hopes

It was exactly this kind of propaganda which those who wanted war with us put about in Japan. No country has been more held up in Japan as a model of success than we have been; the young Japanese has frequently been told the lessons of British patriotism in the past, but in some magic way we are supposed to have lost all this, and to be easy meat these days. There were a lot of people who thought this way in Europe, and even in America, four or five years ago. They no longer share this view, and it may be that Gen. Tojo is the only one left who does. It is already clear that if we have lost all our money in the European war, we have gained in reputation to a degree which may outbalance it. When we have shown the Empire that nothing could be allowed to count in the scale against the preservation of decency as we see it, and not till then, we shall have overthrown the most serious assault ever made on civilisation and have overthrown it in just that way which our enemies have maintained that we would not—by the exercise and strengthening of just those qualities which the Japanese say we have lost. Even they will not deny that we once possessed them.

WAR

The Philippines

ABCA 'War' Pamphlet No. 89, March 3rd, 1945

S.W. PACIFIC

We'll Be Back

By Capt. F. E. FIRMINGER, A.E.C.

WAR *Staff Writer*

What Do We Want to Know About the American Land and Sea Battles of the Philippine Islands?

Does it bring the end of the war within sight?
How was it done?
Why was it done?
What are the Filipino reactions?
What part did the British Empire play in it?
What is the next move?
How do the Japs like it?

That should be enough for the moment. Let us try to put them in some sort of logical order, and see whether we can help to find the answers.

1. WHY WAS IT DONE? This requires that we should look at a map, and for this purpose the map in Map Review No. 55 will do. The reasons for making an attack on the Japanese in Luzon and the other Filipino islands will probably be clear to all.

2. HOW WAS IT DONE? This should take us into a quick re-view of the steps leading up to the invasions on Leyte, Mindoro and Luzon, and an account of the campaign up to the fall of Manila. We shall have to look at the problems to be overcome, and the manner in which they were in fact disposed of.

3. WHAT PART DID THE BRITISH EMPIRE PLAY IN IT?
This will need no more than a statement of the British Imperial
Forces deployed under General MacArthur's command, and an
account of what they did. We shall try to keep proper perspec-
tive of the various parts played.

4. WHAT ARE THE FILIPINO REACTIONS? Here we shall
have to say a word about the Filipino leaders and the Quislings,
what the Japs have done during their occupation, and about
U.S.-Filipino relations in general both before the war and after.

5. HOW DO THE JAPS LIKE IT? It won't be spoiling the story if we say now that they don't like it at all, but we shall have to
give an idea of just how and why they don't think that anything
particularly good has happened to them.

6. WHAT IS THE NEXT MOVE? This will be guess-work, but
it is always popular to work out the High Command's next move
and to compare our guesses with the later events.

7. DOES IT BRING THE END OF THE WAR IN SIGHT?

This is also a matter of guess-work, but it will involve our
summing up the situation in the Far East as a whole, and perhaps
comparing it with the state of affairs two years ago.

1. Why Was It Done?

Get a Map

For this question it is essential to have a map, and ABCA Map
Review No. 55, although it is illustrating a different campaign,
sets out to illustrate the same point, which is the vulnerability of
Japan's communication system. From this it will emerge that the

attack on the Philippines cuts Japan's newly acquired Empire in half, and in particular divorces the main islands of Japan from the South Seas.

What does Japan get from the South Seas? *Rubber, petroleum, tin, manganese and a host of other vital war materials.*

The Dagger at the Heart

Furthermore, the possession of the Philippines brings the Allied Forces very much nearer the heart of Japan. The Japanese have often described the Philippines as a dagger thrust at the heart of Japan, and it has always been the chief ambition of Japanese expansionists to take them from the U.S. or from the Filipinos themselves as soon as their independence from the U.S. had been finally carried out. It might have been supposed that the Japanese would have exerted every effort within their power to defend the islands, and that the campaigns should have been on a far greater scale even than they have been. Does the event show the bankruptcy of Jap military and naval strategy? Were they unable to oppose the American landing with insuperable force, such as is elsewhere in the Far East at their disposal, because of their inability to produce a military plan that would bring the necessary amount of force at the right place, at the right time? Or does it mean that the Japanese took so poor a view of their chances there that they have decided on a defence much nearer home? The narrative of events may help us to answer these questions, but at this stage we may consider certain factors.

AIR POWER, COMBINED WITH SEA POWER, HAD EXERCISED A DECISIVE INFLUENCE ON THE EVENTS OF THE PRECEDING TWELVE MONTHS.

Trouble between the Jap High Command and the Government, between their Army and Navy, may be read into the political events in Tokyo during the months preceding the invasions.

PSYCHOLOGICALLY, THE JAPS WERE BEING HANDED PERSISTENTLY SOMETHING THAT HAD

NEVER ENTERED INTO THEIR CALCULATIONS, AND SOMETHING FOR WHICH THERE HAD BEEN NO PREPARATION—DEFEAT, LARGE-SCALE, UNRELIEVED, AND PROGRESSIVELY WORSE.

2. How Was It Done?

The fear in most people's minds was that Japan had established a formidable array of obstacles between the Allied bases and the homeland, each one of which would have to be separately reduced in long and expensive campaigns before the U.S. forces could get to grips with the main Jap armies. The process was known as "island-hopping," and was regarded with horror, as all the innumerable islands of the South Seas spread out before the map student, and the persistence of Japanese defence on such of them as had been tackled, was taken into account. The Japs, beyond doubt, relied on this.

General MacArthur's hops were much larger than had been thought possible.

The first blow was at Guadalcanal, where one of the first two decisive checks was imposed on the Japanese; the other was the Australian advance in New Guinea.

The Approach from the South

August, 1942.	Landing on Guadalcanal by U.S.
Aug.-Dec., 1942.	Six naval battles of the Solomon Islands. **Japanese fleet forced to withdraw.**
February, 1943.	Japanese evacuate Guadalcanal.
August, 1943.	U.S. take Munda airfield (New Georgia). Japanese evacuate New Georgia.
September, 1943.	All New Georgia Group in our hands.

November, 1943.	Landings at Empress Augusta Bay, Bougainville.
December, 1943.	Landings in New Britain.
February, 1944.	Green Islands occupied. Campaign for Solomons over. Isolated Jap garrison holds out in Bougainville.
February, 1944.	Admiralty Islands.
April, 1944.	Bismarck Archipelago under Allied control, but Japanese garrisons hold out.
May, 1944.	**End of New Guinea Campaign.**
September, 1944.	Halmahera. Allies now dominate the Moluccas.

Thus in two long years of bitter fighting the Japanese had been thrown back from their advanced positions. In the South-West Pacific campaign it is estimated that Japanese forces of 250,000 were destroyed or rendered impotent.

The Approach from the East

	Parallel with this had been the advance over the Pacific from the East.
November, 1943.	Tarawa, Makin and Abemama occupied.
February, 1944.	Truk attacked.
	Guam, Saipan and Tinian attacked.
March, 1944.	**Occupation of the Key atolls in the Marshalls completed.**
July, 1944.	**Saipan fully occupied.**
August, 1944.	**Guam occupied.**
October, 1944.	**Palau Islands occupied.**

The second prong of General MacArthur's and Admiral Nimitz's attacks was now completed, and the Philippines were threatened from two directions. From the south, the Americans had reached Halmahera; from the east they were in the Palau Islands. It needed no expert knowledge at all to guess that the next blow would be in the Philippines, but when it came, the Allied force achieved such possibilities of surprise as were left to them by the selection of Leyte.

The Punch at the Centre

October, 1944.	Air assault on Formosa.
	Landings on Leyte. Tremendous air assault prevents Jap reinforcements from reaching Leyte, where the Jap force is only 20,000 out of nearly a quarter of a million in the Philippines.
	4-DAY SEA-AIR BATTLES PUT JAP FLEET OUT OF ACTION.
	Samar occupation complete.
November, 1944.	**Air assault continues.**
December, 1944.	**Fall of Ormoc.**
	Landing on Mindoro, virtually unopposed.
	Campaign on Leyte closed. In the fighting and the attempts at reinforcement, Jap casualties (dead) put at 90,000. Air Assault on enemy airfields maintained.
	Landing at Lingayen Gulf.
January, 1945.	**Capture of Clark Airfield.**
	Further landings.
February, 1945.	**Americans enter Manila.**

From these events, what salient points can be observed?

The inability of the Japanese to interfere effectively with American plans.

The immense effort involved in the supply aspect of the campaigns.

The taking of the strategic centres and the by-passing of others. Compare with the by-passing of such places as Poznan by the

Russians, remembering the far worse position of the Japs, who are unable to play any part at all in the campaign which has swept past them. They are contained by sea-air power in narrow sea-bound limits, whereas the by-passed Germans have road connections on the ground and have to be mopped up soon, before they can make damaging sorties.

The Jap Military Balance

Certain things have been imposed on the Japanese without reference to the way that they feel about it. What are they?

To fight on several fronts. Burma, China, Philippines and the South Seas.

To disperse his force, sea, land and air, with the result that an Allied task force can approach Tokyo.

To observe, without being able to lift a finger to help, **his own assets wasting** in a score of isolated spots which have no hope of ever seeing again a ship, a plane or a parcel of stores marked with the Rising Sun.

The Inner Ring

The physical effect of this was to bring the U.S. forces inside Japan's Inner Ring. The psychological effects were no less disastrous to the Japanese. For the first time there creeps into the Jap soldier's thoughts the idea of defeat. Not yet defeat in the war as a whole, but defeat in the little locality for which he was responsible. There begins to emerge, too, an awareness of the crushing steam-roller power of Allied total mobilisation.

Trouble in Tokyo

At home, the adventurer Tojo was swept away and replaced by General Koiso as Prime Minister, with Admiral Yonai as his chief collaborator. This was the strongest cabinet which the Japanese can expect to produce, and to the Japanese it is a measure of the dire

THE PHILIPPINES

circumstances which surround them, much as the War Cabinet which Mr. Chamberlain, Mr. Ernest Bevin and Mr. Churchill all found it possible to join was an indication of the difficulties which faced us. For Koiso was the leader of the Japanese who believe in war and the divine mission; a secret and powerful figure whose influence in the army was probably greater than that of any other general. Admiral Yonai probably disagrees with every idea that Koiso has ever had, except for the necessity of doing something to get Japan out of the hole in which she now finds herself.

Relaxation of Army Control

Furthermore, Machida joined the Government. He is the one politician of power in Japan, and he had steadfastly refused to join former Governments. He is probably against the war, but accepts it as something which cannot now be helped. The result of his entry was a series of promises of concessions in the way of freedom of speech, and a more general participation of the people as a whole in the government. It could only have been brought about by the force of powerful, and unfavourable, events outside the control of Tokyo.

Scores of Thousands at a Blow

But all this did not produce a successful policy for the halting of the American drive. "We shall destroy the enemy with one annihilating blow," screamed Koiso. This annihilating blow, killing scores of thousands of the enemy at one attempt, is a favourite theme of Japanese soldiers. Their difficulty was to get themselves in a position to deliver it. The invasion of the Philippines was clearly foreseen, but in the sea-air battles around the coasts of the islands, the annihilating blows were the ones delivered by the Americans. The scores of thousands of dead were Japanese, and the Japanese garrisons on the islands had to be left to manage as well as they could without decisive reinforcements from home.

Let us summarise the steps which made the invasion possible.

1. The approach from the South and East to positions from which vast forces could reasonably be dispatched towards Leyte.
2. The destruction of Jap air-sea power in the area.
3. The confusion caused in Japanese minds by the mounting lists of defeats. This may have been accompanied by sharp disagreements between their army and their navy.
4. The landing on Leyte, and consolidation there.
5. The landings on Luzon, and the capture of Manila, involving the division and defeat of the forces at General Yamashita's disposal.

3. The British Empire's Part

The Australian force which participated in the Philippine invasion was the R.A.N., consisting of the cruisers *Australia* and *Shropshire*, the tribal class destroyers *Arunta* and the *Warramunga*, with the support of H.M.A. ships *Kanimbla*, *Manoora* and *Westralia*.

The operation took a heavy toll of Australian personnel, including the Commanding Officer of H.M.A.S. *Australia*.

Apart from these specific Australian ships, and Australian air units, the creation of the new British Pacific Fleet bases on Australia will have a major effect on the already acute Japanese naval anxiety.

Japanese propaganda had sought to make light of the British promises to see the war out in the Far East with the same degree of effort that had been made in Europe. Nobody expected major British forces to be taken from the various European theatres of war, but the creation of fresh power specifically for the Far East was an important political event.

The Whole Picture

At the same time, the year of victory in Burma had been

achieved by forces which were preponderantly British, Indian, African and Chinese, and presented to the Japanese the threat of a vast link-up with China, which was second only in disastrous potentialities to the Japanese to the thrust at the heart which came from General MacArthur and Admiral Nimitz.

4. What Are the Filipino Reactions?

The Philippines may be taken as the geographical centre of the Far East. Operations are more conveniently directed towards the East Asiatic mainland, towards the Dutch East Indies or towards Japan itself from them than from any other one place. Formosa is only 225 miles from northern Luzon. There are nearly 200 known airfields, two naval bases and many natural harbours.

The Philippines and the Filipinos

The population is 16,000,000.
They are not self-supporting in food. There is a food shortage on the islands, with crisis in the cities.

Iron, copper, chromite, manganese, gold, silver, are the chief metals.

The population is chiefly around the coasts of the larger islands.
They are 80 per cent. Roman Catholics.
English is very widely spoken.
There is still a ruling class, but a middle class is emerging.
It is estimated that they are 95 per cent. loyal to the U.S.

An Example of Benevolent Working

The Japanese, aware of the Filipino dislike for them, made strenuous efforts to clothe their intentions with a picture of self-government.

The "new republic" was inaugurated on 14th Oct., 1943. The Japanese have always held up the Philippines as an example of the benevolent working of their plans for East Asia.

In fact, the "New Constitution" was conspicuously in every way less independent than the former Commonwealth Constitution.

Japanese "advisers" now filled the departments. Only minor posts were left to the Filipinos.

The Executive Commission under Vargas (former secretary of President Quezon), which nominally ruled up till the "new constitution," made strenuous efforts to deal with the widespread chaos caused by the war. But in effect the Kalibapi (pro-Japanese mutual admiration society) ruled behind the scenes. On 14th Oct., 1943, the Kalibapi made Laurel President. A former Yale student he had been Secretary of the Interior before the war. He is very little short of a dictator in his power to appoint half of the National Assembly and to veto. He can, and did, with these powers, give the Japs anything they wanted. What they wanted was everything the Filipinos had, or could produce. Their exploitation has been thorough-going and ruthless, and their departure is marked by all the usual signs of chaos and inflation.

The Real Leaders

The U.S. had, of course, continued to recognise as much of the pre-war Government as got away from the islands. Until his death, President Manuel Quezon, a lifelong fighter for the independence of the Philippines, unhesitatingly supported the American plans. After his death President Osmena, who is part Chinese, carried on, and landed with General MacArthur with some of the first units ashore. Osmena had been Quezon's chief opponent on internal Filipino issues, but was his staunchest collaborator in face of the threat from Japan.

In spite of the tendency for some Filipinos to have accept-ed the situation after the Japanese capture of Manila, and to have carried on as best they could without active hostility to the Japanese (which is very much easier to talk about than to achieve) it is thought that the effect of the Japanese occupation is to have united the islands as never before. It is proposed to hand over the mopping up of Japanese forces left there after the main battles to the Filipinos themselves. While it is too early to talk of the activities of Filipino irregulars during the occupation, it will later be found that they were in every way to be compared with the most virile movements in Europe.

5. How Do the Japs Like It?

"Naturally Japanese"

That Japan should own the Philippines was considered in military circles in Japan to be a "natural" course of events. On cinema screens in Japan where educational films on the rest of the Far East were popular, it has been reported that for years a shadow has been allowed to fall on the maps of the Philippines of the same sort that marked off Formosa and other Japanese possessions from the rest. It is not that the Philippines have much that Japan wants, but that they were a group of islands off the Asiatic coast, and to the Japanese it seemed slightly indecent that there should be such things outside of their control.

When Japan took the Philippines from the U.S. after Pearl Harbour, the loss of face* suffered by the U.S. was considered great. The corresponding loss of face to the Japanese is that much greater now that they have in their turn to see themselves turned out. For in matters of face he who laughs last laughs very much longer, and the one who lost at first, only to come back later, has on the whole benefited in a net estimate of the account. The co-prosperity sphere is no longer a tactful talking point for the Jap.

Cutting the Co-prosperity Sphere

Apart from these points of morale, the military significance can hardly be over-estimated. In hostile hands, and in the con-

---

* "FACE" is an oriental expression peculiar to Japanese and Chinese which may be rendered into English as meaning a form of self-respect.

dition of modern war, as the Americans wage it, they are indeed a dagger thrust at the heart of Japan. Moreover, to the East Asia Co-prosperity Sphere, their fall into the hands of the U.S. is very much more disastrous, for from the Philippines the cutting in half of the whole area is assured.

THE JAPANESE HAVE MADE NO SECRET OF THE SERIOUSNESS OF THE BLOW. THE "ASAHI" NEWSPAPER, THE TIMES OF JAPAN, SAID: "*The Battle of the Philippines has entered a decisive stage and holds the key to the entire war in the Pacific.*"

GENERAL YAMASHITA COULD DO NO BETTER THAN THIS: "*The loss of an island or two in the Philippines does not matter. We shall allow the enemy to advance and then annihilate tens of thousands of them at one stroke.*"

Hon. Situation Grave

When the Diet met on January 21st Koiso declared that Japan was faced with the gravest situation since the outbreak of the war in the Pacific, and that her fate hung in the balance. There were many who felt that just as the loss of Saipan had put an end to Tojo, so the fall of Manila would bring Koiso down, but it may be doubted whether there is any other combination that Japan would make which would look any better to the Japanese public than the present set-up.

Hon. Deep Sympathy

From Admiral von Saalwachter came a German estimate of what had happened, for the Japanese to derive what consolation they could. Apart from the threat to Japan's communications, the Admiral mentions:—

1. A considerable intensification of the air war against Japan proper.
2. Improvements in the American supply traffic.

3. Greater facilities for the major repair of damaged warships.
4. Eventual landings in Japan proper.

None of this will be news to the Japanese public. For years their expansionist apologists have been using these arguments as a reason why the U.S. should abandon the Philippine Islands. They are familiar to every schoolboy who remembers his lessons on the spiritual mission of Japan.

6. What is the Next Move?

Looking at the Map on page 192 (S.W. Pacific), what prospects open up as a result of the fall of the Philippines? Answers may be:—

A direct blow at Japan proper.
A landing on Formosa.
A landing in China.

Straight for Japan?

The reasons which will finally determine the American choice are of course not open to the examination of one and all. In the first flood of optimism there are plenty of people who look for a bound straight for the southern islands of Japan proper. The Americans have shown that this kind of adventure is well within the bounds of conservative possibility in their sort of war. A reckoning of distances, and a comparison with what has so far been done will help, however, to show the gigantic nature of the task. If this is the method chosen, will it be combined with a thrust from the north, from Kiska and Attu?

Honourable Desperation

Where is the Japanese Navy? What is left of it would have to come out if General MacArthur takes this road. They would at any rate be able to fight at an advantage in having shore-based aircraft nearer at hand than the Americans would have, but the Americans have shown a singular ability to overcome these disadvantages, and the means to which the Japanese now resort— the suicide pilots—are the means of desperate men who have abandoned hope in their ingenuity and material, and fall back on a total disregard of human standards. Which is the more remarkable, that Japan should have young men prepared to give their lives in this way, or that she should find herself saddled with leaders who have to ask it of their men?

WHAT ARE THE ADVANTAGES OF TAKING FORMOSA?

Further closing Japan's communication system.
Getting even closer to Japan's main islands.
Making major landings in China possible, and threatening Japan's land link with her southern conquests.

An Essential Step!

The optimists who see the road to Japan open without more ado will no doubt point out that the possession of Formosa may be regarded as a luxury in the business of cutting Jap communications. If they look closely at the map of China they may see further difficulties even after the landing has been made on the China coast in the mountains that have to be crossed beyond. But the more conservative-minded may feel that the step closer is an essential one, even if no attempt is yet made on the China coast. Some may think that the whole of Japan's forces in China might be by-passed on the road to Tokyo in the same way that the island garrisons of the south have been left behind. In which case we should have the interesting phenomenon of defeating a major military power without meeting in the field the greater part of its armies. This is just the sort of record which Americans like to hang up.

This is all speculative. The reasons which finally decide the choice which has no doubt already been made cannot be appreciated without information which will not be available till the end of the war.

7. Does It Bring the End of the War In Sight?

What are some of the points for?

1. The Americans have run rings round the Japs at their pleasure. There seems to be no reason why they should not continue to do so.

2. *The interruption in Japan's supply of material must be vital. Though we have seen in Europe that Germany has been able to struggle on after an interruption at close quarters on a scale which can hardly be hoped for yet in the Orient.*

3. The fact that they cannot win the war must be growing slowly more apparent to more and more Japanese.

4. *The time for the deployment of vast British forces seems near.*

And now for some points against.

Only a Beginning

We have not yet encountered the main Japanese armies. This has been due to the fact that American air-sea power has been able to keep reinforcements at a healthy distance. Can this continue?

The Japanese have shown no sign of abandoning their last man and last round methods of defence which inevitably make their final destruction a longer business.

Tremendous though the leap into the Philippines has been, the leap to Japan proper is a lot longer.

The invasion of Japan proper, quite apart from the distance, may be a very different business from the invasion of other places in which the Japanese were less numerous and less fiercely interested.

Japan Itself as a Target

It is not supposed that this exhausts the list of possible points for and against, but they are some typical examples of the sort of considerations around which discussion might develop.

To sum up, we have seen part of the reasons why the Philippine Islands were a major target, and the steps which made it possible. We have seen the part played by the British Empire in the campaign. We have seen in the Filipinos a people ready for full independent self-government, offering many comparisons with people within the British Empire. The Jap in defeat, and Japan itself as a target for Allied arms, have been new considerations in the gradual unfolding of the war.

Japanese Army Quiz

1. Who is the Japanese Commander-in-chief in the Philippines?

2. For what operation was he formerly the most famous?

3. How are Japanese ranks indicated on their uniforms?

4. Who was the Japanese Prime Minister at the time of the re-entry into Manila by the U.S. Army?

5. What is the big difference between the Jap War Minister and our own in his position in the government?

6. On all Japanese soldiers' various head-dress there is a symbol. What is it?

7. Who was Colonel Hashimoto?

8. Who said "We shall annihilate tens of thousands of them at a blow?"

9. How can you distinguish the Japanese soldier's arm of the service?

10. What is the chief weapon carried by Japanese officers not carried by British officers?

11. What association does the Japanese word KAMIKAZE have?

12. What is the Japanese private infantry soldier most likely to have been in civilian life?

13. What are first steps to be taken on taking a Japanese prisoner, before sending him to the rear?

14. What is the Kwantung Army?

15. What do the Japanese mean by "personal punishment"?

16. The average age of Japanese Generals is higher or lower than in the British Army?

Answers overleaf

Japanese Army Quiz:

ANSWERS

1. General Yamashita. He is aged 59 and is known to be strongly pro-German. He was former Inspector-General of Aviation.

2. The capture of Singapore.

3. By a patch on both sides of the collar, which are red with various stars for privates, and a combination of stars over thin yellow stripes for N.C.O.s. For officers there is a gold patch with various combinations of red stripes and stars.

4. General Koiso.

5. The Jap War and Navy Ministers are not responsible to the Prime Minister and the Cabinet as a whole, but directly to the Emperor, so that they need not fall with the Government of which they are members.

6. A five-pointed star.

7. A retired officer who suddenly appeared at the head of troops in Central China in 1937 and sunk the British gunboat *Ladybird* in the hope of precipitating war between Great Britain and Japan. He is also the most notorious secret society leader in Japan.

8. Any Japanese commander about to suffer a defeat and not having the slightest idea what to do about it.

9. By chevrons of different colours worn on the right breast. The colour gives the arm of service—red for infantry and tanks, yellow for artillery, black for Military Police, and so on.

10. The two-handed sword, which he will also commonly use in action.

11. It means "divine wind" and is the name chosen by the Japanese suicide pilots to differentiate their squadrons.

12. A farmer.

13. Make it impossible for him to destroy any marks of identification on his uniform or papers in his possession.

14. The crack Japanese Army based on Manchuria, a largely independent force from the rest of the Japanese armies.

15. Personal punishment is the universal practice of any Japanese soldier higher in rank than another administering corporal punishment on the spot to his inferior.

16. Much higher. It is very common for a Japanese commander to he in the middle sixties.

WAR

The Road to Rangoon

ABCA 'War' Pamphlet No. 96, June 9th, 1945

The Road to Rangoon

By Major ERNEST WATKINS, R .A.

WAR Staff Writer

THE ultimate objective of every military commander is to destroy the capacity, and the desire, of the enemy nation opposed to him to continue the fight. That is an obvious statement, but it is important to keep it in mind when thinking of the campaigns in Burma. Our ultimate object was not the recapture of Burma. That was only one of the objectives in a campaign that had as its target the islands of Japan, some 3,000 miles away. Rangoon is a stage on that road, but the Burma phase has been concluded, with success.

The situation in Burma 12 months ago was in a state of crisis. May, 1944, saw the Japanese advance at its zenith. Imphal had been virtually surrounded. Kohima, over 60 miles to the north, and well into India, was invested and the Japanese had cut the road between Kohima and the Indian railhead at Dimapur. If they had reached that railway not only would they have captured an important supply base, they would also have cut the link that supplied the other road into Burma, the new road that ran south from Ledo and which we hoped ultimately to convert into an effective link with the interior of China.

The Japanese Never Recovered

But by July the situation had been reversed. No longer had the Japanese the initiative. The five Divisions that had reached out into Manipur had been defeated. Kohima and Imphal had been relieved and the road between them cleared. Further east an additional stretch of the Ledo road had been retaken, Mogaung captured and Myitkyina invested. The gain of territory was not considerable, compared with the total area of Burma still to be cleared, but the Japanese Army had been decisively beaten. In fact the Japanese Army in Burma never recovered from that defeat.

The campaigns in Burma have been dominated, not only by the ground and the jungle, but mainly by the weather, the monsoon period. That starts late in May and continues to the following November. Last July the Allied Commander, then, had in front of him two differing weather periods, first, the next four months, the balance of one monsoon period, and, second, the succeeding six months, when Central Burma would be dry and suitable for a war of movement. The second six months, too, would be a period when air power could be used to the best possible extent.

Hinged on the Question of Supply

The next problem to be settled hinged on the question of supply. Supply rests on ports and the facilities there available for the onward movement of the stores landed at them. So far, two ports had been in use, Calcutta, in India proper, and Chittagong, on the borders of Burma. Both could handle ships of from 5-6,000 tons, both had rail communications and both were good bases from which to supply the area along the North-West frontier of Burma. But neither had any direct communication with Central Burma.

The next port down the coast was Akyab. This also can take ocean-going ships and before the war had a considerable export trade in rice. It was a regular port of call for British India vessels. But there was only one road over the Arakan range into Central Burma and that was usable only in dry weather. Finally there was Rangoon, the major port in Burma.

Rangoon, then, became the final objective for 10 months ahead. Once that was in our hands, we had advanced nearly another 2,000 miles from Calcutta. We had a base from which operations could be mounted either south or east, or in both directions, and we were well placed for the liberation of Malaya and the nearer sections of the Dutch East Indies.

The Answer must be Air Transport

But until Rangoon was taken the problem of supply to Central Burma required another solution. It was impracticable to carry southwards from Imphal a road that would adequately supply the whole 14th Army in active, mobile operations in the valley of the Irrawaddy. There was no through railway. The country was a series of mountain ranges, deep valleys, thick jungles and, in the monsoon, fantastically high rainfall. The answer must be air transport.

That meant air bases as close as possible to the ports and it meant, too, that first the Japanese Air Force in Burma must be reduced to impotence.

But it would be impossible to get to Rangoon by the end of May, 1945, if a start was postponed until after the end of the 1944 monsoon. It was necessary to move south from both the Imphal and the Myitikyina areas before then. If possible we had to be clear of the jungle-covered hill country that fringes the whole of the northern and western flanks of Burma, by the end of the year. On the north, if possible, we should have got to Indaw and Bhamo. On the west we should be along the line of the Chindwin River and as far south as Kalewa. Kalewa is the real gateway between Burma and India. Eastwards from Kalewa the heavy jungle is left behind. Although it is still hilly to the south, to the east the country opens up and movement becomes possible.

Plan for Ten Months

In the dry season, Central Burma is a comparatively level open plain of paddy fields, so dusty that one jeep will raise a cloud of dust that can be seen 20 miles away, but admirable for mobile

warfare as in the Western desert of Africa. We must be poised on the edge of this plain, ready to strike when the rains stopped.

In short, then, the plan required the dovetailing together of a number of very different operations.

1. Central Burma

To the north-east the Chinese would push down the old Burma road towards Lashio. In the north the line of advance lay towards Bhamo and Indaw, to reach the Irrawaddy and the railway line south to Mandalay. The column next to the west would advance along the general line of the Chindwin river and start moving east when they reached the neighbourhood of Kalewa. They should then be able to make direct contact with the columns to their east, and together be well placed for the capture of Mandalay. After Mandalay there were two routes to the south, one the direct line along the railway, through Taungoo and Pegu to Rangoon. The other lay to the west down the valley of the Irrawaddy proper through Prome (terminus of another railway from Rangoon) to Rangoon.

2. Arakan

At the same time the Akyab area must be secured, first to eliminate any threat by the Japanese there to Chittagong and, more important, to provide a further port and base for air operations.

That operation must be timed so that the port and base were available at the end of the monsoon period. They were not necessary until then. Flying was difficult over the mountains in monsoon weather, while the ground there made it very difficult to lay out landing strips, or, indeed, DZs, for dropped supplies. But once the open plains were reached supplies could be landed at will and would be needed without delay.

3. Sea and Air

And it also meant that in the two months of flying weather from the end of November to the end of January the offensive power of the Japanese Air Force in Burma would have had to be destroyed. As the transport of supplies in unarmed merchantmen at sea is dependent on command of the sea, so the transport of supplies in unarmed Dakotas is dependent on command of the air.

... And Rangoon Before the Monsoon

Operations that have to be fitted into such a strait-jacket timings as these are not always successful. The remarkable thing about the 1944-45 Burma campaign is that it was completely successful. Rangoon was reached on 3rd May, fourteen days before the monsoon was due.

Time Table for Ten months

Here is a time table of the principal dates:—

1944

AUG.-SEP. Progress was made down both the two routes south into Burma, the pace being determined far more by the difficulty in making a supply road than by the strength of the enemy opposition. By the end of September the position on the east was that patrols were within 25 miles of Myitkyina, in the west we were approaching Tiddim and preparing to assault the naturally strong defensive positions in the Kennedy Peak area, some eight miles south of Tiddim. A patrol link was made with the Chinese troops operating on the north-eastern frontier.

★ ★ ★ ★ ★

OCT. Progress in miles was slow during the month. In the west the Japanese still held the Kennedy Peak-Fort White positions in the Tiddim area, but forces had been pushed south beyond them in an outflanking movement and had reached as far as 47 miles south. In the east progress was made down the road to Bhamo.

★ ★ ★ ★ ★

NOV. In the west Tiddim was taken, and its defending positions, Kennedy Peak and Fort White, by direct assault, including tanks (they fought above the cloud line), and the way opened for further and more rapid movement east. In the east Chinese troops advanced southwards far enough to cut the railway between Bhamo and Katha. Improvement in weather made air operations more possible and fighter sweeps over airfields in Central Burma began on an increasing scale. Operations on land in the Arakan area began with patrol activity southwards in the general direction of Akyab. Main Japanese resistance in the Bhamo area.

★ ★ ★ ★ ★

DEC. Kalewa, on the Chindwin river, was taken on the 2nd, in the east Bhamo was finally cleared and Indaw and Katha occupied, and in the Arakan area Buthidaung was captured. The stage was now set for the assault on Central Burma with the New Year, and the end of the monsoon.

★ ★ ★ ★ ★

1945

JAN. The month opened with two opposed crossings of the Chindwin by troops of 33 Corps, the first by 19 Div, north of Kalewa, who then struck due east to the Irrawaddy, the other by 2 and 20 Divs, who pushed through Shwebo and on to reach the Irrawaddy below Mandalay at two points between Mandalay and the confluence of the Irrawaddy and the Chindwin. In the north 36 Div and the Chinese troops under command of SEAC cleared the upper Irrawaddy and linked up with the Chinese troops from China, to clear the Ledo-China road, so that on the 23rd, Admiral Lord Louis Mountbatten was able to send the following signal: "The first part of the orders I received at Quebec has been carried out. The land route to China is open." On the Arakan section, Akyab itself was taken on the 2nd, on the 21st a landing was made on Ramree Island, and on the 26th on Cheduba. On the 18th the first road convoy from Ledo entered China along the Burma Road.

★ ★ ★ ★ ★

FEB. In the Central Burma area, the month saw the start of the encircling movement that destroyed the Japanese armies defending Mandalay. 19 Div established a bridgehead over the Irrawaddy from the west north of Mandalay. The remainder of 33 Corps established another to the south-west of the town and the second was exploited during the month to the extent of cutting the branch railway from Thazi to Myingyan just south of the latter town. In the Arakan area operations proceeded to clear the vast swamp area lying between Ramree Island and Akyab.

★ ★ ★ ★ ★

MAR. This month saw the conclusion of the battle for Mandalay. The major event was an armoured thrust west from the Irrawaddy by 4 Corps, south-west of Mandalay, to capture Meiktila and cut the main Mandalay-Rangoon railway at Thazi. This was heavily counter-attacked but held its ground. In the meantime Mandalay was attacked from the north and Chinese troops worked round to the east. In the Arakan area the Japanese were in full retreat and a further landing handicapped their withdrawal on Taungup.

★ ★ ★ ★ ★

APR. This month saw the drive on Rangoon. By the 10th 4 Corps were already 100 miles south of Mandalay and going fast down the railway, while the area to the south of Mandalay was being cleared. 33 Corps were going down the Irrawaddy valley. Taungoo fell on the 24th. In the Arakan area Taungup was taken on the 3rd, and the Japanese abandoned Sandoway.

★ ★ ★ ★ ★

MAY. To ensure the capture of Rangoon intact, a combined air and sea attack was launched from the south on Elephant Point, a few miles below the port. A Gurkha parachute battalion was dropped on the 1st and a seaborne force came in on the following day. On the 3rd Rangoon was entered, 4 Corps then being only a few miles to the north. By the end of the month the position was that the line of both the railway and the Irrawaddy were held, with one Japanese force pinned in the south-western area of Burma awaiting liquidation and the remainder in full retreat to the east in the Shan Hills.

The Japanese were Completely Overtopped

An operation that goes with such a clocklike precision, while not exactly suspect, sometimes tends to attract the comment that the other side couldn't have been very good at their job. It is true that the Japanese were outgeneralled and outfought, but no one, least of all the Japanese themselves, would claim that they are not a warlike race. On the contrary, it was the British and the Americans who were the degenerate interlopers in the Far Eastern Sphere of Co-Prosperity. And the Japanese soldier fought with his accustomed suicidal violence. It was in the field of generalship and organisation that the Japanese were completely overtopped.

Nor did the Japanese voluntarily give up command of the air. It was in the air that the combined effect of all the Allied

THE TIDE IN THE PACIFIC TURNS

JAPAN & annexed territory shown in black

Limit of Japanese advance ━━━

RUSSIA

MONGOLIA

CHINA

MANCHUKUO

KOREA

Vladivostok

KURILE IS.

JAPAN

TOKYO

BONIN IS.

VOLCANO IS.

IWOJIMA

Feb. '45

PACIFIC OCEAN

WAKE

Apr.'45

OKINAWA

FORMOSA

SHANGHAI

FUCHOW

HONG KONG

HAINAN

LUZON

PHILIPPINES

Oct. '43

SAIPAN Jun. '44

GUAM

YAP

PALAU

CAROLINE IS.

TRUK

MARSHALL IS.

Sep.'43 July '44

GILBERT IS.

MIDWAY

30°

Pearl Harbour

HAWAII

JOHNSTON

15°

0°

Chunking

INDO-CHINA

SIAM

BURMA

RANGOON

MALAYA

SINGAPORE

SUMATRA

BORNEO

TARAKAN

JAVA

MACASSAR

TIMOR

DUTCH EAST INDIES

NEW GUINEA

SOLOMONS

CORAL SEA

MELANESIA

NEW HEBRIDES

FIJI

AUSTRALIA

INDIAN OCEAN

CEYLON

INDIA

ANDAMAN IS.

NICOBAR IS.

PHOENIX IS.

SAMOA

45° 30° 15°

0 200 600 1000

Miles

Bip Pares

15°

30°

45°

0°

15°

operations against Japan was most felt. Not only was its fighter strength being attacked by the Allied Air Forces in Burma. It was also being shot to pieces in the Philippines at the same time, with the result that units were withdrawn to fight nearer home, urgent replacements never came, and the final state was that the Japanese were faced with Allied fighters practically sitting over their airfields waiting to shoot down any aircraft that attempted to take off, while freight aircraft of S.E. Asia Command (of which 60 per cent. were R.A.F. and 40 per cent. American) were flying something like 15-16,000 sorties, carrying some 18,000 tons of stores and 14,000 passengers and casualties, each week.

Bled White in the Pacific

And the same at sea. There had been a time, in 1942, when the *Prince of Wales* and *Repulse* had gone, that the Japanese thought they had seen the last of the British Fleet. Yet three years later the Japanese could not muster a single surface craft to give any opposition to the landings along the Arakan coast. Their naval strength had been bombed in Singapore and bled white in the Pacific.

Yet the land campaign was nothing like as uncomplicated as an exercise, although an exercise in such a country would be an appalling task to organise and administer. There are the crossings of the Chindwin and the Irrawaddy. There are the operations around Mandalay.

The Irrawaddy is not an easy river on which to make an opposed crossing. It is twice as wide as the Rhine at Wesel, and every item of equipment had either to be improvised on the spot or carried some 600 miles over a jungle road or flown up in a freight aircraft. And this was the situation around Mandalay at the end of January.

Slim's Union Jack

On the north, 19 Div were coming due south on the west

bank of the Irrawaddy, Mandalay itself lying to the east of the river. Just south of Mandalay the river turns west, flows due west for some 30 miles and then turns south-west to its confluence with the Chindwin, and the rest of 33 Corps was in that bend. The Japanese regarded the Irrawaddy as something approaching a Maginot Line.

19 Div crossed it, in the face of heavy opposition, north of Mandalay and drew some of the Japanese strength in that direction. 2 and 20 Divs then made another crossing west of Mandalay and secured a bridgehead. That bridgehead was not expanded. It was a bait and the Japanese threw two Divisions against it, but since the bridgehead was designedly small and was covered by virtually a Corps concentration of artillery on the other bank, that area became a killing ground and the attacks failed.

General Slim then executed what he called his "Union Jack" operation. 4 Corps came in the west, striking across and slightly to the south of the front held by 33 Corps, and made south-east for Meiktila, to reach, and cut, the Mandalay-Rangoon railway. 33 Corps, leaving a Division to mop up Mandalay, followed this blow by striking south-west down the Irrawaddy itself. The movements of the two Corps were like an enormous pair of scissors cutting the Japanese positions to ribbons and they succeeded completely in that task. From Mandalay southwards there was no organised Japanese Army in Burma. There were just a great many Japanese soldiers trying to make their way eastwards towards Siam.

As an example, the record of 4 Corps may be summarised. By May, 1945, it had been fighting against the Japanese for three years with only 10 weeks in rest. During that time it had advanced 732 miles, destroyed or captured 57 tanks and 511 guns and killed 31,800 men.

● *The above account deals more particularly with operations in Central Burma. Here, from a naval angle, is an account of the Arakan front, to the west.*

Hide and Seek among the Mangroves

THE amphibious operations which have enabled Lieut.-General Sir P. Christison's XVth Indian Corps to expel the Japanese from the greater part of Arakan are noteworthy from several points of view. Perhaps never before—not even in Normandy in June, 1944—has naval co-operation exerted such a direct influence on land operations.

Sloops have worked as river gunboats, taking up bombardment positions in mangrove swamps 30 miles inland. Destroyers have engaged Japanese troops and gun emplacements while lying at anchor within 50 yards of enemy territory. B-type Fairmile motor-launches have been used offensively on a scale unknown in any other theatre. Minesweepers and landing craft have "blockaded" Japanese-occupied areas and engaged (with 3-inch, Oerlikon and Bren guns) enemy motor-launches and canoes engaged in trying to evacuate Japanese troops through inland waterways. An island, 150 square miles in extent, has been occupied by Royal Marines of the East Indies Fleet, supported by cruiser and destroyer bombardment and carrier-borne aircraft—the first all-naval landing of the war.

The story of the campaign begins in October, 1944, when Naval Combined Operations Pilotage Parties and soldiers and marines of a Special Service Brigade began a series of raids and reconnaissances at various points on the west coast of Burma.

Persuade the Enemy to Weaken

These raids had a dual purpose. They enabled us to gather

information about suitable beaches and the nature of the defences, which was essential to the planning of later assaults. They also helped to persuade the enemy to weaken his land front in Northern Arakan and reinforce the coast farther south. The raids were supplemented by a series of "pin-prick" bombardments by the M.L.s.

These "pin-pricks" were actually rather sharp when administered by a force of up to five coastal craft blazing away for 15 or 20 minutes at a range of half a mile with 3-pdr., Bofors, Oerlikon, Vickers and 3-in. mortar. Frequently such bombardments drew fire from 37-, 75-, and 105-mm. guns and the heavy mortars which are favourite weapons of the Japanese, who use them with uncanny skill.

The raids and bombardments had the desired effect. The Japanese fell back from the Mayu River valley and evacuated Akyab Island. A Commando Brigade and an Indian Brigade landed unopposed on the northern shore of the island on 3rd January, 1945, and the port of Akyab was occupied the following day.

The Japanese Expected Us

The use of Akyab as an advanced base for our landing craft reduced by at least half the distance they would have to cover to reach the Myebon Peninsula and Ramree Island—our next objectives. Akyab had been the air base from which the Japanese had carried out sporadic raids on the docks at Calcutta and Chittagong. It now became an advanced R.A.F. base from which fighters could give the Fleet complete air cover in later combined operations.

Nine days after the "bloodless" assault on Akyab Island, another invasion fleet was crawling, through the night, past the Barongas and across Hunter's Bay to a lowering position a few miles south of the Myebon Peninsula, which is 32 miles east of Akyab. The Japanese expected us here, and preliminary reconnaissances had shown—on the very beach where we proposed to land—about

100 tree-trunks embedded upright at regular intervals below low-water mark. These were dealt with.

The R.A.F. laid on an impressive air strike, while the *Narbada* and the *Jumna* sent salvo after salvo crashing into the beach defences. The first wave of R.I.N.* assault landing craft, with Commandos on board, touched down at 0830, and although Japanese 75s, mortars, machine-guns and land mines inflicted a certain number of casualties, a workable beachhead was soon established.

It Will Take Them Just Twenty Minutes

Later in the day, some difficulty was experienced in getting tanks ashore from the LCTs.† The first one off sank in the soft mud of the river bank and, before the majority could be coaxed on to dry land, the Japanese 75s got the range. Shells fell so thick and fast all round the LCTs that they had to pull out and land the rest of their tanks under cover of darkness on a more suitable beach. When these guns stopped firing, a Royal Artillery observer on the bridge of the *Narbada* said: "It will take them just 20 minutes to shift their guns round and make the necessary calculations to have a crack at us." Sure enough, during the twentieth minute a shell landed in the engine room of H.M.M.L. 381, lying alongside the *Narbada's* port quarter. Miraculously, there were no casualties and not even a fire, although the port engine was smashed and the electric wiring of the engine room was torn to shreds.

As the Commandos were now firmly dug in, it was unnecessary to maintain such a concentration of naval craft in the Myebon River and give the enemy some gratuitous target practice, so the *Narbada* hoisted a plain-language signal which read "S-C-R-A-M," and with the M.L.s‡ and LCTs then withdrew to Hunter's

---

* R.I.N.—Royal Indian Navy.
† LCT—landing craft, tank.
‡ M.L.—motor launch.

Bay, where the *Phoebe*, the *Jumna* and the rest of the "invasion fleet" were lying.

A Two-way Squeeze was Beginning

The object of the successful landing on the Myebon Peninsula had been to get astride the enemy's line of communication and encircle five Japanese battalions between Myebon and Mychaung. A two-way squeeze was beginning, with the 81st West African Division pushing down the Kaladan valley from the north and the 25th Indian Division, which followed up the Commandos, pushing up the Myebon Peninsula from the south. There was still, however, a gap to the east through which ran the main Japanese line of communications running northward from Taungup.

Arakan coastal forces now set about severing the water transport route, while the sloops began shelling the road. A permanent block was established in the bottleneck by M.L.s, which were relieved every 12 hours. The block was most effective. A number of Japanese diesel-powered landing craft, carrying food, ammunition and petrol, were intercepted at night and destroyed by gunfire.

The block was maintained until our troops had got astride the overland supply route by a landing south-west of Kangaw on 22nd January, The Japanese had more than a brigade at Kangaw and some of the bitterest fighting of the whole campaign ensued.

Anchored Close to a Minefield

Meanwhile we were maintaining the momentum of our southward advance. On 21st January, nine days after the Myebon landing, the biggest combined operation of the campaign was successfully carried out at Ramree Island, 35 miles farther south. Some 6,400 British and Indian troops were carried to the lowering position in LSTs.*

So effective was the combined naval and air bombardment

---

* LST—landing ship, tank.

that opposition on the beach was negligible and our troops were not seriously engaged by the enemy until the afternoon. In the meantime, however, we had discovered that the fleet was anchored in close proximity to a minefield. A fully loaded LCA* blew up and when H.M.M.L. 891 came in to pick up survivors she, too, struck a mine and disappeared in a great pillar of flame and smoke. There were, however, only three fatal casualties.

A remarkable feature of these two explosions was the experience of an Army officer who was going ashore in the LCA. He was blown into the water, picked up by the M.L., blown up a second time, rescued, and taken on board the *Rapid*. The first thing he saw when he reached the destroyer's quarter-deck was his own kit, which had been salvaged intact. He went ashore later, none the worse for his adventurous passage, and not even short of a toothbrush.

Five days later (26th January) we made another 50-mile leap to land 475 Royal Marines on Cheduba Island.

I Think I See a Horse

As this was the first all-naval landing of the war, H.M.A.S. *Nepal* brought Vice-Admiral Sir John Power over from Ceylon to see the show. When the *Nepal* hoisted her Australian Battle Ensign, H.M.M.L.s 391 and 437 (manned by the Burma R.N.V.R.) took it to be the cue to hoist their own national flag—a peacock in his pride displayed on a Blue Ensign. The Royal Marines, who were being led in to the beach by the M.L.s, were quick to notice this and gave the Burmans a cheer and the "thumbs up" sign. The operation was not without its traditional touch of good humour. A signal was passed from a destroyer to a cruiser, saying: "I can scarcely believe my eyes, but I think I see a horse on your quarter-deck." The cruiser replied: "Reluctantly compelled to deprive colonel of his steed, due to lack of space in boats." The destroyer had the last word: "Send boat for hay."

* LCA—landing craft assault.

The Royal Marines held Cheduba Island for five days, until relieved by troops of the 26th Indian Division. Meanwhile other troops of this division had made appreciable progress on Ramree Island and there were indications that the Japanese intended to pull out across the mangrove swamps to the mainland.

Secured Alongside the Mangroves

It was then decided to "blockade" the island in order to prevent the Japanese from joining up with their comrades on the mainland. The destroyers were supplemented by motor minesweepers, M.L.s and LCAs (carrying Gurkha Bren-gunners). These craft patrolled the channels between the island and the mainland by day and secured alongside the mangroves at selected points to watch for enemy movement at night. Every inch of the waterways which the Japanese had to cross was thus covered by our guns.

On one occasion the crew of a R.I.N. assault landing craft heard the unmistakable sound of trees being felled, and passed word by R/T to the nearest M.L., which came up in support. After an interval they saw a large makeshift raft being lowered gently into the water not a hundred yards from them. They held their breath—and their fire— until about 50 Japanese had swarmed on to the raft; then all guns opened up together.

Too Narrow to Allow Evasive Action

On the 20th February the Army estimated that the naval blockade had so far written off 286 Japanese, of whom only three were taken prisoner.

By now the Japanese in the Mychaung-Kangaw area had been mopped up. The next assault was made at Ru-Ywa. Another squeeze developed, this time with one Division pushing southward and another driving eastward. The importance of this move may be judged from the fact that only 75 road miles separate this point from Minbu and Magwe, on the Irrawaddy.

The Japanese had a great concentration of artillery in the Ru-Ywa sector and our sloops, M.L.s and landing craft had a pretty rough time. The chaungs were too narrow to allow them to take evasive action, and uncharted rocks and mudbanks added to the navigational hazards. Practically every M.L. ran aground sooner or later. It was certainly a fantastic mode of naval warfare.

Presented the Ship with a Field Gun

Space does not allow a detailed description of all the minor operations undertaken by the Navy in the past few months, but it can be said that they have been a fine demonstration of Empire co-operation. Sailors from the United Kingdom, Australia, New Zealand, South Africa, India, Burma, Hongkong, and Malaya have worked together in splendid fashion. The Royal Indian Navy has played a great part providing all the minor landing craft (with the exception of a few LCAs and LCSs* manned by Royal Marines), two of the M.L. flotillas and three of the sloops, as well as escort vessels for the invasion convoys.

Nor have the big-ship sailors forgotten their comrades-in-arms ashore who, when all's said and done, have a tougher job than we have in fighting the jungle as well as the Japanese. The *Napier*, when she was about to leave the Myebon area, packed all her remaining canteen stores and sent them ashore to the troops. As a mark of the soldiers' gratitude and their appreciation of her good shooting, Major-General Wood, commanding the 25th Indian Division, presented the ship's company with a Japanese field gun which his men had captured.

This account is reprinted abridged from the Admiralty Weekly Intelligence Report, by permission.

---

* LCS—littoral combat ship (US).

WHITE PAPER ON BURMA

Publication of the Government's proposals on the restoration and the future of the civil government in Burma has followed closely on the heels of the liberation of the major areas of the country. They are published as a White Paper (Cmd 6635. Price 2d.).

It starts with a few facts about Burma. 262,000 sq. miles, a population of nearly 17,000,000, of which the Burmese proper form nearly 66 per cent. of the total indigenous section (of the non-indigenous the Indians, with 1,000,000, are the largest and the Chinese, with 150,000, next), and an economic structure of which rice cultivation is the backbone, are the main points. Rice fields made up 70 per cent. of the total cropped area and rice accounted for £18 million out of a total export trade of £40½ million in 1939/40. Oilfields produced £10 million of products per year. The third major industry is timber. Two-thirds of the population are dependent on agriculture.

Before 1937, it says, Burma was a province in the Indian Empire, but in April, 1937, the Government of India Act, 1935, came into operation. The governmental machine set up under that Act consisted of a Governor, a Council of Ministers, a Senate and a House of Representatives. The franchise for election to the Lower House was fairly wide, including approximately every taxpayer (20 per cent. of the population). They elected 91 out of the 132 seats, the remaining being reserved for minorities and special interests. Half the Senate was appointed by the Governor, half by the Lower House.

In some matters the Governor has to follow the advice of the Ministers (who were responsible to the legislature), in others he has follow his individual judgment. The latter class include some of the major responsibilities of government, such as foreign affairs, financial stability, rights of minorities, etc.

Finally, there was one Section of the Act, 139, which enabled the Governor to take full control if government could not be carried on under the Act. The Governor took action under this Section on the Japanese invasion.

The White Paper then deals with the future. Government by the Governor under Section 139 will continue for another three years, till the end of 1948. A new Government under the 1935 Act cannot be set up until there is a general election and the Government feels that it is impossible to hold a really effective election until the disorganisation caused by the occupation is cleaned up. But, while the Burmese control of government will not be formally working before 1948, it is proposed that the Governor shall increasingly bring Burmese men and advice into the actions he is taking.

Nor will self-government for Burma stop at the level of the 1935 Act. When that is in full effect again the next phase, "the attainment of full self-government," will begin. It is hoped and intended that when the people of Burma have agreed on the type of government most suitable for Burma, full self-government within the British Commonwealth can be established in Burma proper.

CURRENT AFFAIRS

Pacific Enemy

ABCA 'Current Affairs' Pamphlet No. A99, July 14th, 1945

Pacific Enemy

By Capt. C. L. Wayper, A.E.C.

1. THE JOB AHEAD

ON December 7th, 1941, Japan attacked Great Britain and America. In one of the swiftest campaigns of history she overran one of the most powerful empires of the world. Burma, Malaya, the Philippines, the Dutch East Indies, Guam, and innumerable Pacific islands fell before the devastating onrush that stopped only on the frontiers of India and Australia. At Singapore Japan inflicted upon us "the largest military disaster in British history." At Pearl Harbour she damaged every capital ship of the U.S. Pacific Fleet. It is a shock to realise that the country which did all this was only a hundred years ago a small, feudal community living in such strict isolation that for any of her people to attempt to establish communication with the outside world was an offence punishable by death.

Rapid development

A few generations ago Japanese were fighting with bows and arrows. To-day they are civilised enough to fight with battleships and aircraft-carriers. A hundred years ago Japan's economy was essentially agricultural. To-day she is one of the world's leading industrial powers, employing in her factories almost as many people as are employed in the factories of this country. Fifty years ago Japanese technicians studied in America and England; Lancashire was the home of the Japanese textile industry. Just before the war the boot was on the other foot. Delegations from Lancashire visited Japan and paid handsomely for the use of Japanese textile patents which were superior to the methods in use in this country. If there are few things in the history of war to equal the speed with which Japan overran so extensive an area, there is nothing in the history of peace to equal the astounding way in which she telescoped into less than three generations a process of development for which we in the west required centuries.

It's them or us

Japan's Pacific conquests gave her nine-tenths of the world's supply of rubber, two-thirds of the world's tin and huge supplies of crude petroleum, tungsten, tea, sugar, rice, phosphates and almost all the available supply of quinine. Were we to give her time to develop these tremendous resources she would become the unconquerable empire she dreams of being. She could flood the world markets with the cheap products of her slave labour. Not only would our own standard of living suffer from such a permanent loss, we would not even win peace for ourselves, for Japan is out for world domination. It is them or us.

The Japanese menace must be removed, you may say, but is it our job? After all, we have been fighting this war two years longer than the Americans. Isn't the Pacific their show? They have done so well there already. Can't they finish it off? No. Apart from the threat to our own way of life and standard of living we have a score of our own to settle with the Japanese for Hong Kong and Singapore, for the *Prince of Wales* and the *Repulse*.*

---

* HMS *Prince of Wales* and HMS *Repulse* were sunk off the coast of Singapore by Japanese aircraft on December 10th, 1941.

We must work with the Dominions

But the account we have outstanding is not only with the Japanese. We are greatly indebted to Australia and New Zealand, Canada and S. Africa. It is natural to think first of the Pacific Dominions as the Japanese threat has been so close to them. Twice in one generation their sons have travelled to the ends of the earth to help us in the day of our need. Shall we leave them in the day of theirs? Canada, our oldest Dominion, has a score of her own to settle with Japan, to avenge the Canadian Brigade lost in Hong Kong. We sometimes forget that she, too, is a Pacific Dominion, and that her security is also menaced by the Black Dragon of Japan. South Africa may seem less concerned with that danger; yet we occupied Madagascar to forestall the Japanese.

Apart from the British Commonwealth of Nations, there is no future for Great Britain as a Great Power, and there is no surer way of dissolving the Commonwealth than by hesitating to play our part in the Pacific war.

—and the U.S.A.

Nor are we unmindful of that other great debt that is not yet settled. Without America we should not have won the European war; without her we shall not win the peace. As Mr. Churchill said: "Upon the fraternal association and intimate alignment of policy of the United States and the British Commonwealth and Empire depends more than on any other factor the immediate future of the world." Failure on our part to co-operate with America in the Far East would be to jeopardise the future of Anglo-American relations.

2. KNOW YOUR ENEMY—It has not been easy

Know your enemy is always a wise council in war, though rarely one easy to follow. It is particularly difficult to know this enemy. Nevertheless, by making the attempt now we will be contributing to Japan's defeat.

Until recently Japan had been very remote from us. She was "our gallant little ally" in the last war, but, for all that, we knew very little about her. Japan was so distant that it wasn't even news. It is only comparatively recently that Reuter has established its own agency in Japan. Until then it relied on a Japanese news agency, which, of course, told us what Japan wanted us to believe, rather than what was actually the case.

To the difficulty of remoteness, we must add that of language. Few westerners have mastered it. Added to that, no nation has carried secrecy to greater lengths than the Japanese. Making such good use of spies themselves they were security minded long before this war. Special police looked after every alien. Too inquisitive journalists disappeared, or committed suicide in mysterious circumstances, both in Japan and in the Pacific Islands from which their long prepared blows against America and Australia were to be delivered, and which, of course, as Mandated Territory were not supposed to be fortified. In nearly every way the Japanese succeeded in their intention of keeping us ignorant of the real nature of their designs.

Jekyll and Hyde on a national scale

Remoteness, language, secrecy are real obstacles to an understanding of Japan. There is another, perhaps greater than any of these, the Japanese people themselves. They seem so contradictory, so complex. They have a natural courtesy and a delicate love of beauty that has captivated most observers. They indulge in such simple ceremonies as moon gazing when whole families will meet at the full of the moon and sit on the veranda enjoying its beauty, or long sessions of flower-gazing. Yet they are capable of the most revolting cruelty and bestiality as at Hong Kong, Singapore, Manila and Nanking. The grace of their women is

They seem so extraordinarily complex

world famous, yet they are subjected as in no other great country to-day. The "Yoshiwara" is extensive and flourishing. Peasants sell their daughters into prostitution as a recognised way of eking out the family income. Whole districts, such as Niigata which is renowned for the prettiness of its girls, send much of their young womanhood to the brothels of the towns. They are a powerful twentieth century people waging modern war, yet they see nothing absurd in announcing that "an artificial eye factory is now busily engaged in making a giant glass eye which will be offered to the Kwannon Temple at Asakusa to console soldiers who have lost their sight in the China affair."

The key to the contradictions?

The Japanese have made a fine art of sending off to the Western Powers notes of apology or denial, sometimes even despatching the notes before arranging the incidents for which they are apologising or denying. Yet they appear genuinely shocked and hurt when their good faith is impugned. They have committed act after act of aggression, the Sino-Japanese War, the Manchurian affair, the Chinese incident, yet their speakers in the Diet can cite these very acts as proof that Japan's policy is a policy of peace. What are we to make of such people?

The interpretations we have had of Japan usually give us one side of the picture only. Either the Japanese are depicted as sub-human, capable of any excess, or they are seen as a people apart, dwellers in a flowery world, in the land of the Lotus, the Land of the Rising Sun, the Land of a Thousand Luxurious Reed Plains. However, neither of these interpretations is wholly satisfactory. We must try to get some more composite picture of the Japanese.

3. JAPANESE RECIPE—First, Shinto—the way of the gods

The Japanese flag portrays the rays of the rising sun. It is difficult for us to realise that in the twentieth century a people as advanced as the Japanese can believe that their royal dynasty is descended from the Sun Goddess, and that the Japanese, in general, are descended from gods of some kind. Until we grasp this fact we cannot begin to understand the character of Japan. Belief in their own divinity is the beginning, the middle and the end of Japanese mentality. Undisturbed by the views of humorists such as the Chinese, who say that centuries ago they collected all their criminals and sent them off to Japan, where they mated with monkeys and apes and the Japanese people resulted, belief in their own divinity is one of the strongest of Japanese beliefs and is one of the most important influences that have moulded their way of life.

The Japanese called it "Shinto," which means the Way of the Gods. That is to say the Japanese are one of the most arrogant and conceited of all peoples. It is nothing for one of their leaders to say "From the fact of the divine descent of the Japanese people proceeds their immeasurable superiority in courage and intelligence over the natives of all other lands."

It's that "Herrenvolk" myth again

The Germans have taught us in the west what racialism means. Here is another, even more extreme, instance of it. The parallel between Germany and Japan is astonishingly close. The Germans claimed to inherit the earth because of their superior Nordic blood: the Japanese because they are gods. It is clear that Shinto is as dangerous as the doctrine of the Herrenvolk. In the hands of a few men obsessed by the lust for world domination, it is a mighty instrument for evil. If

"The parallel between Germany and Japan is astonishingly close"

you believe you are divine you will not be too reluctant to impose your divinity on the rest of the world. It is your right, indeed your duty, to do so. It is no accident that over the leading Shinto shrine in Japan is to be found the inscription: "Hitherto there have been Japan and foreign lands. Mark it well all of you. Hereafter shall be naught but Japan."

An old tradition in modern dress

Before leaving Shinto, the Way of the Gods or racialism, we must notice two things. There is much that is modern about it. Only recently has so much been made of it, shrines repaired that had fallen into disuse, every facility used—school, factory, army, press, radio and cinema—to drum it into the people.

But if Shinto were merely the result of a recent propaganda drive we would still have a tremendous task before us, the problem

U · S · S · R
MONGOLIA
MANCHURIA
SIN-KIANG
Mukden
Peking
Vladivostok
SAKHALIN
KURIL ISLES
HOKKAIDO
KOREA
JAPAN
Tokyo
Osaka
Nagasaki
KYUSHU
CHINA
Nanking
Shanghai
TIBET
Chungking
INDIA
BURMA
Hongkong
FORMOSA
RYUKYU Is
OKINAWA
BONIN Is
MARIANAS
SAIPAN
GUAM
HAINAN
FRENCH INDO CHINA
SIAM
Rangoon
Bangkok
Saigon
LUZON
Manila
PHILIPPINE ISLES
PALAWAN
MINDANAO
PALAU Is
TRUK
CAROLINE ISLANDS
Brunei
SARAWAK
Tarakan
Singapore
MALAYA
SUMATRA
BORNEO
CELEBES
HALMAHERA
NETHERLANDS INDIES
JAVA
TIMOR
NEW GUINEA
Aitape
Port Moresby
SOLOMONS
CORAL SEA
INDIAN OCEAN
AUSTRALIA
0 1 2 3 4 5 1000 2000
SCALE IN MILES

so admirably summed up by Cardinal Newman when he said: "Give me a child until he is seven, you can do what you like with him after that, you will never alter the ideas I have put into his head." Unfortunately Shinto is not just a modern development. We hear of it from earliest recorded Japanese history, and the curious thing is that although Japan has borrowed some of the great ethical and religious systems of the world, her primitive native beliefs have never been supplanted.

Thus it would be dangerously wide of the mark to think of Shinto as exclusively a modern belief. Its strength is that it appeals to ideas with which the Japanese have been familiar for centuries.

Secondly, Kodo—way of the Emperor

If you want to conquer the earth, it isn't enough to believe that you are a nation of gods. After all, gods are singularly in-disciplined creatures. Their activities on Olympus, for instance, or in Valhalla, were neither seemly nor serious, and though they are mighty warriors they are far too individualistic to form a conquering array. Thus the Japanese must see that the individual godhead doesn't matter and that it is the collective godhead alone that counts. The individual is nothing, the State is everything and the individual must be prepared to sacrifice everything, even life itself, in the service of the State.

It's an Asiatic version of "Prussianism"

In racialism we have one very close parallel between Germany and Japan. Here in this doctrine of the omnipotent State, we have another. The Germans have this belief. We call it Prussianism, the view that the individual exists for the State and not as we hold that the State exists for the individual. The Japanese share the German belief. They call it Kodo, which means "The Way of the Emperor."

We have seen the importance of Shinto, the Way of the Gods, in launching Japan upon her path of world conquest. Kodo is equally dangerous in that it has welded individual gods into one disciplined, cohesive whole, acknowledging no god higher than the Emperor, knowing no morality other than reasons of State. It is the social cement that has held the Japanese together in evil courses, just as Prussianism is the social cement that has held Germans together in evil ways.

The legend of the Son of Heaven

Kodo really only emphasises the Emperor-worshipping aspect of Shinto and in that sense is a modern development. A good illustration of the modernity of this cult of the Emperor is the change in his official title. Until 1936 he was known simply as the Emperor of the Nation of Japan. After 1936 he became "Great Japan Imperial Son of Heaven." It is only recently that such a tremendous propaganda drive has been made to convince the people that "the Japanese Emperor is the personification of the whole race, not an individual." Some years ago the American magazine "Time" published a Japanese supplement with a portrait of the Emperor as frontispiece. The editors were asked to request their readers to treat this particular number with all due deference and above all not to place anything on top of the Imperial features.

Unthinking loyalty is the foundation

Loyalty to one's overlord, unflinching and absolute, is one of the most pronounced characteristics of the Japanese people throughout their history. Indeed, they have come to regard loyalty and obedience as the supreme virtues. Thus the traditional conflict in Japanese drama is that between a man's natural affections and the loyalty he owes to his overlord. An overlord is distressed for want of money. His vassal must help him and the only way in which that is possible is by selling his wife into prostitution. He does so and is acclaimed as a model of virtue since the principle of loyalty has triumphed over the affections of the flesh. More convincing proof could not be required of the evil lengths to which the Japanese are prepared to take their notions of loyalty or of the truth of the old saying that the corruption of the best is the worst.

These notions of loyalty, it is clear, are the very firmly built foundations of Kodo.

Kodo emphasises Emperor worship.

Thirdly, Bushido—way of the warrior

If you wish to conquer the earth it is not enough to believe you are a nation of gods, nor to believe that the individual must sacrifice everything to the State. You must develop the fighting services and inculcate the fighting spirit.

In militarism, which Japanese call Bushido, or the Way of the Warrior, there is, as in racialism and Prussianism, a striking parallel between Japan and Germany. Many have wondered how the Japanese could reconcile atrocities with their much vaunted doctrines of Bushido. Such bewilderment reveals a fundamental misconception of Bushido. It is not like chivalry which taught protection to the weak and mercy to the vanquished. It is a code of the conduct to be observed to one's superiors—not to one's inferiors, and it preaches steadfastness even to death in battle. In its modern dress it stresses that the Imperial uniform must never be disgraced and that "to die for the Emperor is to live for ever." The Three Human Bombs, three soldiers in the Shanghai fighting who draped themselves with H.E. and carrying a bomb hurled themselves against the Chinese emplacements, are held up as the perfect example of Bushido.

How it works

A good illustration of Bushido is the well-known Japanese attitude to capture in war. As a diary taken from a dead Japanese soldier put it—"For a Japanese to be taken prisoner is not only a personal disgrace, it is the greatest dishonour that can befall his whole family."

Though modern propaganda has undoubtedly done much to spread the doctrine of Bushido, it is clear that that doctrine is nothing new to the Japanese, but is based upon their traditional virtues of loyalty and obedience.

If, as the Japanese Army claims, it is the only army in the world which teaches men not so much how to fight as how to die, its teaching could never have been so successful but for the whole background of Japanese history, but for Shinto and Kodo, and the twisted, warped mentality they have produced. Like Shinto and Kodo, Bushido or militarism, is an odd mixture of the old and the new, and like them it has been an important factor influencing Japanese mentality.

Summary—they're a tough proposition

These doctrines, put over by all the propaganda resources of a great modern State, helped by hordes of secret police ever alert for dangerous thoughts, helped by hundreds of patriotic societies, all of them indulging to a greater or less extent in political assassination, helped, moreover, by the constant intervention of the army in politics, have produced the enemy we are fighting to-day. It is worth noting that not all these influences, however powerfully backed, have been able to produce all the results desired all the time. During a demonstration organised outside the American Embassy in Japan on the fall of Singapore, a member of the Embassy strolled on to a balcony and cheerily waved his handkerchief at the ravening mob below. The effect of his unexpected action was magical. The Japanese began to titter, began to laugh and cheer, and, in spite of everything that the police could do to get the demonstration started again, the mob broke up and dispersed in high glee. Nevertheless, it is clear what the general effect of such pernicious teachings must be, and the Japanese soldier is a fanatical, tough and formidable proposition.

4. HOW THEY GOT THAT WAY— They've been isolated

Why have the Japanese developed such fantastic ideas? Two main reasons, isolation and contact with the West will help us here. Take the geographical isolation first. A somewhat misleading comparison is often made between Japan's position off the coast of Asia and our own off the shores of Europe. The Straits of Dover are little more than 20 miles across: the Straits of Tsusima connecting Japan with the Asiatic continent are rather more than 100, and even then the 300 miles of Korea lie between Japan and China. Thus geographical isolation is a factor in Japan's history that helps to account for the peculiar ideas that she has developed.

Mentally as well as geographically

Together with the geographical isolation of Japan we must take into account a certain mental isolation. The Japanese have been great borrowers, but they have always been better at taking over the trappings of civilisations with which they came in contact

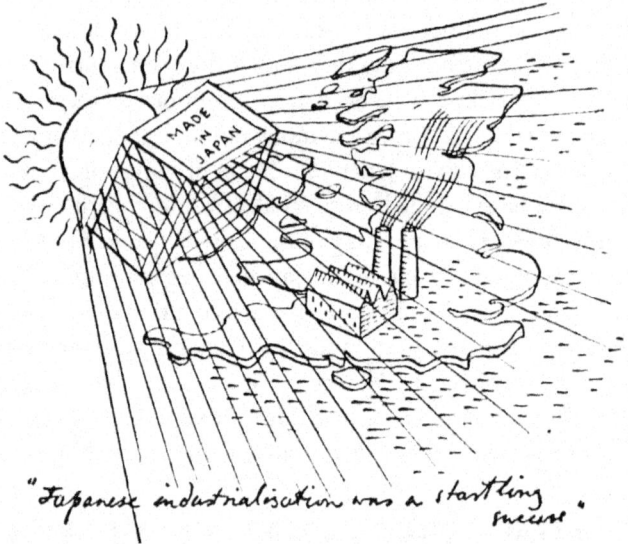

"Japanese industrialisation was a startling success".

than in appreciating their real meaning. Thus, they took script and art forms from China, but never began to understand the great Chinese civilisation. Chinese civilisation was an aristocracy of learning with an Emperor who ruled by virtue and who could be deposed if his virtue was not apparent. Japanese civilisation was an aristocracy of birth with an Emperor who ruled by biological right as being the direct descendant of the Sun Goddess.

Alarmed by the spread of Christianity, the seventeenth century rulers of Japan forced their country into a rigid isolation, the like of which has hardly been known in history. Intercourse with the world was forbidden, ships capable of crossing to China destroyed, foreigners expelled, sailors who had the misfortune to be wrecked on Japanese shores executed. For two and a half centuries Japan turned her face away from the new ideas and great discoveries of one of the most formative periods in the history of mankind. It is difficult to exaggerate the effect of this self-imposed isolation.

Contact with the West strengthened their ideas

Even later, contact with the West could not break into this closed circle. When the two and a half centuries of isolation were ended by Commodore Perry's visit in 1853, opening Japan to western trade, oddly enough old ideas were merely strengthened by the new contact with the world. In China the Imperial House opposed westernisation: China soon became a republic. In Japan, because 1868, the year in which modern Japan was born, saw a restoration of the Emperor not a revolution, old ideas of the Emperor's divinity—ideas developed in isolation and never forgotten—received a new fillip. Moreover, the Japanese, suffering from an inferiority complex since the humiliating display of American might which had forced trade upon them, sought comfort in the reflection that they were not as other men—they were sons of gods and gods themselves. Thus, far from meaning the end of Shinto, contact with the West merely strengthened and confirmed traditional ideas.

Chinese fate was an object lesson

The impact of the western world was disastrous for Chinese civilisation. Western traders, missionaries—most of whom were admirable men, but some of whom it could, unfortunately, be said that they came to do good and did well—and soldiers descended upon an unhappy China. Concessions, extra-territorial rights, treaty ports, became the order of the day.

With such an object lesson before her, it is understandable that Japan should fear China's fate and that she should seek to avoid it by acquiring armed force. If Japan's view of western civilisation was a good deal more material than moral there is much truth in her charge that it was the western powers who made it so. Remarkably quickly Japan became powerful. "Little Jap the Giant Killer" defeated the colossus, China, defeated Russia, helped in the defeat of Germany. It is difficult to exaggerate the importance of the fact that Japan has never been defeated in modern war. The inferiority complex became a superiority complex. Japanese had defeated not only China but great western powers—they must indeed be gods. Once again the pernicious doctrines of Shinto were reaffirmed.

The army could always impose its will

The Army, moreover, occupied a peculiar position in the State. It was modelled on the German Army and, like it, was responsible to the Emperor—not to Parliament. This was a fatal weakness in the Japanese Constitution. Japan made an honest attempt to work democracy; in time liberal ideas must have replaced primitive notions of Shinto, Kodo and Bushido. But as the Army was not responsible to Parliament, Parliament could not control it and in the end it controlled Parliament. It became the tradition that the Minister for War must be a serving officer. No officer could be appointed unless by the Army's wish. As no Cabinet could be formed without a Minister for War, the Army could

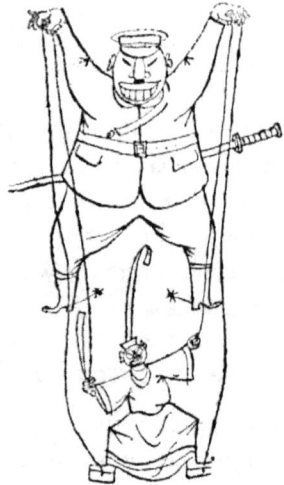

The Army is the power behind the throne —

wreck any Cabinet by refusing to appoint one. Thus the Army could always impose its will, although, as in the 1937 elections, it might only command 66 seats in a house of 466 members.

It was the Emperor's master

The Army was all powerful. In theory the servant of the Emperor, in fact it was his master. It never intended that the Emperor should be more than a figurehead. It was to be the power behind the throne. How well it succeeded we know.

The present Emperor, Hirohito, was educated as a constitutional monarch and in the opinion of the British and American ambassadors to Japan he was opposed to the present war. The failure of the makers of the Constitution to subordinate the military to the civil power thus ultimately led to the extinction of all civil authority, including that of the Emperor, and the scrapping of the Constitution itself.

The problem that faced them—population pressure

In spite of this constitutional weakness democracy might have survived, and the Army been restrained, but for an ever-present problem. In less than three generations Japan had added 40 millions to a population living on an area less than that of California and considerably poorer in natural resources. Her population was increasing at the rate of one million each year—population pressure was a very real problem her rulers had to face. Emigration was no help. Japanese are not good emigrants and the rest of the world did not want them.

Industrialisation will support a large population and with low labour costs. Japanese industrialisation was a startling success. Yet it seemed a policy that would yield diminishing returns. Japan must one day face the competition of India and China where labour costs were less than her own. The world economic crisis of 1930-1 was a sharp reminder that even industrialisation had not finally solved the population problem.

The solution they chose—war

It was now that the Army stepped in with its solution of the population problem—the conquest of raw materials and of markets. Disgusted with democratic ways which seemed to involve national humiliation, as in the acceptance of the famous 5:5:3 ratio in capital ships at the Washington Naval Conference,* and alarmed at the prospect of China growing strong and united, the Army struck in Manchuria and began the process of forcing the hand of the civil authority which ultimately led to the present war and the extinction of that authority. And because the people, too, were aware of the population problem, because they believed, as they had done for centuries that what is in the interests of the State must be right as it fulfils the will of the Emperor who is God, and because the Army seemed so successful, the Japanese people supported it.

Contact with the West had certainly brought liberal ideas to Japan, but those ideas were not strong enough to stand against the forces of the old order, against the ancient traditions which had developed in isolation and which were only strengthened and confirmed by the circumstances in which westernisation came to Japan. Shinto, Kodo and Bushido, it would be true to say, are stronger in Japan to-day than when Perry's "black ships" steamed into Tokio Bay.

---

* It had been decided at the conference (November 1921–February 1922) that the tonnage of naval construction undertaken would be in the ratio of 5:5:3 (US: Britain: Japan).

5. CONCLUSION—When they'e defeated

When Japan is defeated the victorious powers will be confronted with the problem of convincing her that her own interest lies in adopting peaceful ways for the future. This is not simply a matter of ensuring the permanent disarmament of Japan. It will also be necessary to afford her sufficient economic opportunity to feed and clothe the population, but at the same time to make her realise that, only after her system of education has been purged of the pernicious influence of State Shinto, with its glorification of military aggression, will her restoration to the comity of nations be possible.

NAZIS

BRITISH VIEWS ON GERMANY
DURING THE SECOND WORLD WAR

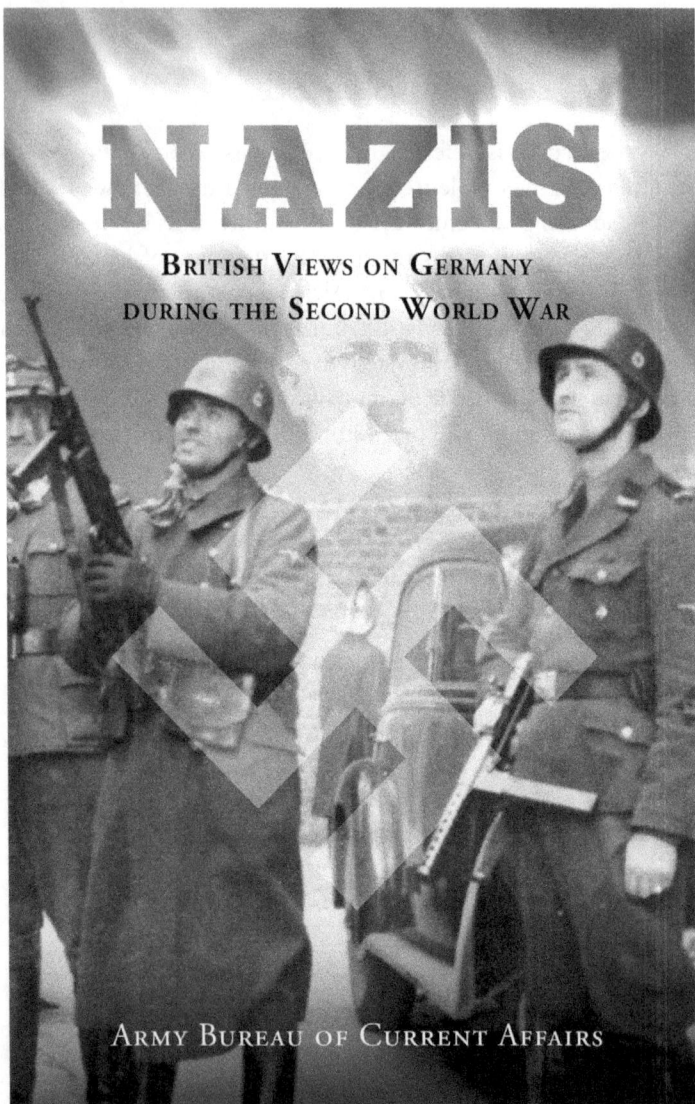

ARMY BUREAU OF CURRENT AFFAIRS

ISBN: 978-1-910375-45-7